Goddess
of
Love

*The Couple's Guide to Unlocking Her Inner
Sex Goddess*

MARISA RUDDER

Author of 15 books and the Best-selling *Love and Obey Female led relationship* Book series.

© 2023 Marisa Rudder.

Available on Amazon Books.

Please contact: Marisa Rudder

Email: femaleledrelationshipbook@gmail.com

Printed in the United States of America Publisher's Cataloging-in-Publication data

ISBN: 978-1-7361835-9-5

DEDICATION

I would like to dedicate this book to all the strong, brave ladies who have joined or about to join the *Love & Obey* movement and live a female led lifestyle and the supportive gentlemen who recognized the natural superiority of females. It is also my desire that women and men experience the joy, happiness, and passion from exploring all aspects of a loving Female Led Relationship (FLR) and understanding all the benefits of loving female authority. If you have not already, please join us on social media. You can find out more at our website:

http://www.loveandobey.com

Or follow me on social media:

FACEBOOK
https://www.facebook.com/femaleledrelationships

TWITTER
https://twitter.com/loveandobeybook

YOUTUBE
https://www.youtube.com/c/femaleledrelationship

INSTAGRAM
https://www.instagram.com/femaleledrelationships

TABLE OF CONTENTS

INTRODUCTION

From the dawn of time, we have been obsessed with a goddess. What is a goddess? A goddess is a woman of great charm and beauty. She is also utterly mesmerizing and has perfected the art of seduction so much so that men become obsessed with her because they experience something magical. I believe that every woman has the ability to become her own version of a goddess. Female deities were worshipped as far back as 30,000 BCE based on Paleolithic figurines, cave paintings, and other archaeological finds in Europe, the Middle East, and Africa.

The Female Led Relationship (FLR) is a perfect opportunity for men to help their Queens step into their power as a goddess. Every woman deserves to be treated like a goddess and women are transformed when they can fully experience goddess life. Divine femininity is within every woman, and when your Queen can experience this connection, it changes everything. Life becomes so much more enriching and exciting. An important part of empowering your Queen is goddess worship, and how well you worship her correctly makes all the difference in your daily life.

This book is going to instruct you on every aspect of goddess life and goddess worship. Do you crave a sex goddess? Do you desire to experience how your Queen can be mesmerizing and create a magical sexual experience? How much more exciting would life be? For several years and in my first 14 books, I have shown couples how to turn average women into Queens. I have also shown couples how to turn egotistical, selfish, patriarchal men into devoted submissive gentlemen who live to love, obey, and serve women. Now, we will explore a whole new level beyond women taking charge as Queens.

This book will show you and your Queen how to create a paradigm shift in your life by learning how to unlock your Queen's inner sex goddess and help her to become a Goddess of Love. You will learn about Divine Feminine energy, goddess worship, Tantric, and so much more. In this book, I will begin to take you on a journey of sexual worship that will transform your Queen into a true goddess.

For years couples have reported to me about the amazing transformation they experienced from switching from a mundane male led relationship to a fabulous Female Led Relationship, which has taken them on a spiritual journey into sexuality that has led them to FLR Nirvana. The concept of Nirvana is associated with spiritual enlightenment and inner peace. To achieve Nirvana, a person focuses on cultivating a spirit of self-discovery, acceptance, and forgiveness. Engaging in activities that bring joy, such as the powerful focus on sexually pleasuring a woman, a couple can reach a state of Nirvana.

Focusing on a woman's sexual pleasure as part of the sacred journey of goddess worship will take your Female Led Relationship to a whole new level. What if the focus went beyond the woman's pleasure first and shifted into a new focus of sexually worshipping your Queen as a Goddess of Love and tapping into the Divine Feminine energy in the universe? What if Divine Feminine energy is channeled through a Queen so that her submissive gentleman could even experience Nirvana with her? To unlock your Queen's sex goddess is to create a paradigm shift in your relationship or marriage. Ancient sexual practices like Tantric sex have long been associated with mystical qualities, such as having the ability to tap into the Divine Feminine energy and power of the universe. Once achieved, you feel peace and harmony through your lovemaking.

Now imagine taking your already fabulous female led lifestyle and transcending into a new female led spiritual realm of goddess worship that can allow you to achieve Female Led Nirvana. This book is the gateway to Female Led Nirvana and will show you the path to building your own personal Shangri-La. Shangri-La has been described as a beautiful oasis of natural beauty hidden in the Himalayan mountains where everyone is joyful and at peace. Now imagine each day of your life feels like you live in your own personal Shangri-La where you and your Queen experience excitement, inspiration, adventure, and of course, sexual satisfaction. You live to worship your Queen, as your Goddess of Love, and she rewards you by sharing her Divine Feminine energy and power.

A goddess can be described as having full of divine energy and power and is discussed in various mythologies and religions. She is often seen as possessing a superpower and strength far beyond that of humans. In some cultures, she is revered as a creator and sustainer of life, a symbol of beauty and femininity. Goddesses may also be seen as protectors, or bringers of luck, fertility, and good fortune. A goddess is connected to the Divine Feminine and all of its cosmic energy and power. Every woman has the ability to unlock her inner goddess and they just need to learn how to do it. A goddess will also desire to have a relationship with a gentleman who can worship her.

In many belief systems, goddesses are believed to have powers and control over various realms or aspects of life, and they can use those powers to stimulate or inspire their men and their followers. Worshipping a goddess can bring positive results to those who do, such as divine protection or blessings. Additionally, goddesses who seek male followers may offer guidance, advice, or rituals in exchange for their worshippers' devotion. Therefore, a gentleman in a Female Led Relationship with a Queen who seeks to become a goddess must learn how to properly worship her and help her unlock her inner sex goddess. Then you both experience all the wonderful benefits of Divine Feminine and goddess life.

Every woman can be a Goddess of Love and step into her power. Fortunately, in the 21st century, goddess worship is on the rise due to a growing interest in the potential healing, transformative, and unique power of the Divine Feminine and a renewed interest in goddess life. Ancient goddesses are often seen as powerful symbols of female strength, and the rise in worshipping these goddesses may be a response to the patriarchal systems of power and norms which have traditionally been in place in many societies. Additionally, goddesses may provide an alternate way of connecting with the divine and understanding the spiritual world, which resonates with many people in today's cultural climate. Furthermore, many modern neo-pagan communities, particularly Wicca and other forms of witchcraft, place a great emphasis on the Divine Feminine and, in doing so, perpetuate the appreciation for goddess worship.

Today, goddess culture is on the rise along with female leadership in relationships and society because it is seen as reflective of strengthening female empowerment and as a means of providing a sense of identity, strength, and inspiration. Women leaders in society, such as female politicians and activists, are leading the charge in promoting awareness and acceptance of the Divine Feminine and its significance. Goddess worship provides an opportunity for women to celebrate the power inherent in the Divine Feminine and in their own lives. Goddess worship celebrates the prized traits that women possess like thoughtfulness, empathy, strength, resilience, and creativity. These traits allow women to make valuable contributions to their families, communities, and societies as a whole.

Women also tend to have strong communication skills, which allow them to effectively collaborate with others and build relationships. Women are often praised for their multitasking abilities and approach to priorities, which can help them achieve success in a variety of areas. Finally, women are often seen as leaders who have the capacity to transform their lives and their communities through hard work and dedication. Goddess worship can allow women to feel connected to their female heritage and their Divine Feminine spirituality, providing an important source of strength and support.

Every woman has the ability to fan the flames of her own goddess fire, unlock her Divine Feminine powers, and become her own unique amazing goddess. I do not need to prove that the feminine divine or the goddess truly exists any more than those who believe in male deities have to prove they exist. It is impossible to prove either to those who are adamantly opposed to their existence. However, I believe that the feminine divine and the goddess are a spirit that flows through all women.

Modern women are releasing their inner goddess through meditation and mindfulness practices. Mindfulness is the practice of being aware of your thoughts and feelings in the present moment and accepting them without judgment. It is a form of meditation that helps to improve overall mental and physical health, reduce stress, and improve concentration. Modern women also embrace their inner goddess when they use natural beauty treatments, engage in spiritually meaningful conversations, connect with nature, reclaim feminine energy and understand astrology, find strength within themselves and their femininity, and appreciate the beauty of their own bodies.

Now is a perfect opportunity for gentlemen to help their women free the goddess within her. In the *Love & Obey* movement, a goddess is a powerful, knowledgeable, superior female who creates a Female Led Relationship or female led marriage and rules over those who live within her family. A goddess is seen as transcendent above the rules of patriarchal men, simultaneously existing outside of a man's world and being fully present and active within it. A goddess is an incomparable, powerful, and all-knowing creator of all human life. She is the ruler of all who live in a female led universe. She is a loving being who responds to the requests and needs of the gentleman who serves her, and she is the source of unlimited energy, mercy, and grace. A goddess is merciful and knows how to rule over a gentleman in a loving female led life.

But let's face it, the patriarchy hates the idea of powerful women and all you have to do is look back in history to see their misogyny. The earliest known accusations of women being witches date back to the 1500s, when the Church and state began passing witch trial acts in several countries. These acts were aimed at punishing women who were perceived as having supernatural or occult powers. In reality, these acts were part of an effort to suppress women's power and influence in society. Women were persecuted as witches regardless of their beliefs and sometimes were even seen as embodying the "evil" aspects of the female spirit.

Goddess worship and witchcraft share a common belief in honoring a female aspect of divine power. Patriarchal men have often viewed women's power and influence as threatening to the traditional gender hierarchy. Women who take on traditionally male roles or who challenge social norms have been viewed as dangerous and have been associated with witchcraft. As such, it is not surprising that men have wanted to suppress women's social power and influence by attributing it to something as insidious as an evil form of witchcraft.

Every woman has a goddess inside her, and she will be transformed when she experiences your goddess worship. Participating in the feminine divine will be your highest privilege and most pleasurable reality. Life is enriched and exciting when you help your Queen to transform into a Goddess of Love and unlock her inner sex goddess.

We are on the cusp of a major paradigm shift. Once your Queen takes charge of her Female Led Relationship, you begin to worship her as a Goddess of Love. You also connect to her Divine Feminine power and energy released through her female orgasm. You will feel the Divine Feminine Power and Energy of the Goddess of Love as she climaxes and beyond. Becoming a goddess is an eventual rite of passage for all women and the Female Led Relationship or female led marriage is the gateway. A female led lifestyle opens Pandora's box. Once you open it, you can never go back, and you will never know what's going to happen next. Each day is a new adventure. An epic erotic adventure for you and your goddess to embark on together.

CHAPTER 1

The Goddess Connection

The Female Led Relationship is an opportunity for you and your Queen to explore the goddess connection. Her pleasure and your ability to help her to unleash her inner sex goddess is your life purpose. It will enrich and give you both the sexual satisfaction you deserve. As her supportive gentleman, it is your responsibility to deliver divine bliss to your goddess and you must be genuinely devoted to loving, obeying, and serving her and putting her pleasure first. The power of love will give you the strength, purity of heart, and connection to the feminine divine to dissolve anything and all that might still be separating you at this very moment from achieving the ultimate cosmic orgasm with your goddess.

So, take a look inside and observe your own present attitude and feelings toward your present female partner and make proper adjustments and give her total freedom. Make the decision: Do you want to commit and make your goddess completely happy, right now? Do you want to make a genuine effort to achieve love, to be obedient to her, and to serve all her needs and bring her pleasure? The Female-Led

Relationship is the gateway for you to explore more than just a great daily life with your Queen. It gives you a chance to improve all aspects of her life, making her a greater leader, a more confident woman, and connecting with her on the deepest level possible.

Oral sex is the pathway to the divine. The vagina and uterus give life, and many believe that it is a connection to the spiritual realm. They are also the center for the female orgasm. Why is this important? Humans are not just physical creatures. We are mental, physical, and spiritual beings, and many times unhappiness in individuals and relationships can stem from the inability to satisfy all parts. As the man in your Queen's life, you learned that it was your duty to ensure your woman feels fully served. In daily life, this is accomplished by doing everything she commands and allowing her to take control of all aspects of your life. Sex and the female orgasm are an extremely important part of your service, and now you will be able to connect to her on levels that no one else can.

In the bedroom, you will now be charged with giving your Queen the ultimate sexual experience by making the sex all about her and placing the focus on her. By doing this, you will gain great pleasure as well, because you will not only feel more satisfied in your own orgasms, but you will be confident that you are solely responsible for giving her the ultimate sexual pleasure. Oral sex and your Queen's pleasure becomes the center of the entire sexual session. You, her submissive supportive gentleman, are the most important person in her life. One of the exciting parts of a Female Led Relationship is sharing as many new experiences in daily life as possible. You are supporting your Queen and goddess on her path to connecting to the Feminine Divine, the Divine Cosmic Force of the Universe. This divine connection will enhance your present relationship and bring a new energy into your life.

Tantric masters have long preached the importance of sexual energy. This is so powerful they use it to transcend. They learn techniques to expand and deepen the orgasm experience. In Female Led Relationship, this is what you are doing for your goddess. Sex becomes the ritual you will perform throughout the entire session to help her have that mind-blowing cosmic experience together with her orgasm. Your sex becomes a ceremony, a celebration of the divine. You become more connected to the universe when you bring your goddess to orgasm, and you too are experiencing the euphoria. In Tantric sex, the male energy is like fire — burning hot and fast, but a woman's energy is like water, it flows. It is this difference that makes female led oral sex so much more complex. You will no longer think of your male ego or your male pleasure.

First, when you make sex about lovemaking and worshipping, orgasms are much easier to achieve and raise oxytocin, which helps combat stress and regulate cortisol in the body. People sleep better, regulate appetite and hormones, and report feeling happy and positive. So, when you focus on your goddess's pleasure, you are improving all facets of her being. You ensure all aspects of her life are fulfilled. Connecting to the divine through sex improves your spiritual connection, which is the most powerful way to be connected. I feel that today, this is the missing link. People have become very dissatisfied with religions and many belief systems, and I believe that this is because we were constantly looking for pastors, priests, or churches to create happiness in our lives.

The spiritual connection to the universe, divine, and God lies within us, so as partners in a union, the responsibility is on you and your Queen to create the happiness you are seeking through the daily activities in your relationship. This is what makes female led so special. The feminine represents Mother Earth. This is one of the greatest powers in the universe. When you unleash this power in your goddess, you open up pathways to improve your lives exponentially because both male and female energy are released.

Einstein once said, "Energy can neither be created nor destroyed." This means that energy is a real and powerful force, ever present. There are some practitioners who believe that we can manifest ourselves through the use of sexual energy. This is part of Tantra teachings, and it is believed that through the harnessing of sexual energy, it is possible to achieve enlightenment. But traditional intercourse where the focus is on the man is much more about releasing energy than building it and harnessing it.

This can only happen through the worship of the woman through oral sex and in so doing prolonging the experience, which then takes both of you to higher levels. Sex goddesses swear by the power of sexual energy. If sexual energy can create life, it can help to manifest great things in your life. I believe that it is the breakdown and lack of sexual connection and thus the connection to the divine center, that is the source of the overall breakdown of the relationship.

As the main supporter and servant to your Queen, the responsibility falls on your shoulders. You will need to create the right experience in which you will use and harness the sexual energy you create with your Queen to enrich the relationship. Why is it the man's responsibility? By nature, men are much more aggressive about sex. So instead of focusing on the sex act, which lasts a few minutes and largely leaves the goddess unsatisfied, you can now create a sexual experience for your goddess which fulfills her on a physical, mental, and spiritual level and leaves her wanting more.

The Female Led Relationship is an opportunity for you and your woman to explore the goddess connection. Her pleasure and your ability to help her to unleash her inner goddess is your life purpose. Another way that you can connect to your goddess and help her to become a Goddess of Love is through female led affirmations. I will delve further into the topic of affirmations and goddess worship in Chapter 20. Affirmations are a primary way in which you facilitate the goddess connection and help her unleash her inner sex goddess. You affirm her superiority and bolster her confidence as your leader through the addition of Tantric sex, meditation, and oral worship in your lovemaking as you help her to connect to the divine. In this way you assist her to make the transformation from Queen to Goddess.

The female orgasm is how you strengthen her goddess connection to the spiritual divine. The goddess connection is so powerful it catapults your Female Led Relationship or female led marriage into a whole new stratosphere, and you will witness transformative changes in your daily life. Every night is a new opportunity for you as the supportive gentleman to turn ordinary sex worship into a spiritual form of female worship and deliver divine goddess bliss.

CHAPTER 2

What Is a Sex Goddess?

The Female Led Relationship is the only relationship in which the man is encouraged to worship his Queen. The Queen is an extraordinary woman who is a mixture of a great leader and a sex goddess. What you must do as her submissive man is to support her through her evolution to becoming the Goddess of Love and a sex goddess.

Many Queens in FLR can be considered a sex goddess. What is the true meaning of goddess? What kind of woman is a goddess? A woman of great charm or beauty. A woman who is adored for her beauty and has perfected the art of seduction that a man's experience with her becomes magical. A sex goddess knows how to give pleasure and enjoy her own pleasure as well making the entire sex session memorable.

What do sex goddesses do differently? A sex goddess turns each day into a sexy adventure. A sexy night starts in the morning and continues throughout the day. From the way she looks at you to how she dresses, she exudes an aura of sexiness. From the scent of her perfume to her words — they all have a lingering sexiness that continues throughout the night. Sharon Stone in *Basic Instinct* can be considered a sex goddess. Do you remember the way she looked at Michael Douglas's character?

The way she conveniently places the mirrored door so he could see her changing and not putting on underwear. The way she crossed her legs to expose herself to the police during an interrogation scene, the way she danced and flirted in the club, and finally the day she seduces and has sex with him, which he described as "The Fuck of the Century." A sex goddess understands setting the sexy scene with the right lighting, music, and food. She knows the right things to say and do to create sexual arousal, and once she has you in bed, you know it's going to be electric.

What does it mean to be a goddess spiritually? Goddess spirituality is the expression of Divine Feminine energies within the universe.

A sex goddess also understands the spiritual side of life and how to merge the sexual with the spiritual. She demands goddess worship and proper worship of her divine center. When your Queen is one with her inner sex goddess, she experiences so many benefits — not only for pleasure but for sexual and overall well-being. It helps connect her with her mind, body, and soul. There's likely a path to more love and intimacy, ultimately improving her ability to express how she wants to be loved.

What sets a sex goddess apart is her ability to really let go and enjoy sex. Men love to see their Queens enjoying themselves and being in the moment, but you must help your Queen to let go and unleash her inner sex goddess flow. A Queen who is a sex goddess is open-minded and confident enough to explore all aspects of sex, and communicate her fantasies, desires, likes, and dislikes to you, her submissive man. You must encourage the exploration of your fantasies together and use each day as an opportunity to bolster her confidence and encourage her to be free to engage in sexploration with you. The more you lift up your Queen and support her evolution into becoming a Goddess of Love, the more every experience is going to bring you closer to each other. Sex goddesses are free to be themselves during sex. They are open to new positions, toys, techniques. She'll genuinely enjoy all aspects of sex and, in turn, you both will experience a transformation in your daily life with a very sex vibe.

Women in male led relationships are always encouraged to provide pleasure but never learn how to demand or receive it. A sex goddess or a Queen in an FLR experiences the opposite. Learning how to be a sex goddess enables them to meet their needs without external validation and consciously relate to their submissive men so that they receive maximum sexual satisfaction. Being a sex goddess can help Queens express who they truly are and what they're about. It gives them the confidence to surrender to the rhythm of their bodies and this, ultimately, extends into other areas of life.

Sex is not a mystery but becomes an essential part of the Female Led Relationship or female led marriage. Anna Simon discussed in a 2005 article the importance of changing the dialogue surrounding female sexuality. The goddess movement and its members encourage finding power in femaleness, which does not have to be masculine to be powerful, and that there is an innate strength in being female that all women and woman-aligned people should be able to feel comfortable in portraying. The goddess movement includes spiritual beliefs or practices emerging predominantly in North America, Western Europe, Australia, and New Zealand in the 1970s.

The movement grew as a reaction to perceptions of predominant organized religion as male-dominated and makes use of goddess worship and can include a focus on women, or on one or more understandings of gender or femininity. Goddess worship is your life purpose and committing to this mission completely transforms your relationship into more pleasure, intimacy connection, and bond. It is through real goddess worship that you will help your Queen to achieve the status of sex goddess and become a Goddess of Love.

The vagina and uterus give life and are a direct connection to the spiritual realm and universal force of life. Both are also the center of the female orgasm. This is important because, as mentioned earlier, humans are not just physical creatures but are mental, physical, and spiritual beings. As the gentleman in your Queen's life, you must do everything she commands and allow her to take control in all aspects of your life. Sexual worship and the female orgasm will allow you to connect to her on levels that no one else can.

You are in charge of giving your woman the ultimate sexual experience by making the sex worship all about her pleasure and placing your entire focus on her. By doing this, you will gain great pleasure and feel a closer connection to your goddess. You should feel more satisfied when your goddess orgasms than with your own orgasms. You should feel confident that you are responsible for giving her the ultimate sexual pleasure. The important part of being a couple in a Female Led Relationship is supporting your goddess on her journey to connect to the Feminine Divine, the Divine Cosmic Force of the Universe. This goddess connection will enhance your present relationship and bring a new energy into your life.

As you facilitate your Queen's journey to become a goddess, you must transform conditional patriarchal love into unconditional love. You must learn to accept her fully and completely as your leader. You will have a loving acceptance of your woman without any conditions or expectations. It is this acceptance that aids in your own transformation. Unconditional love can help bring a sense of comfort, support, and healing to an open Female Led Relationship.

Tantric masters have long preached the importance of sexual energy. The connection between unconditional love and sexual energy is that the experience of unconditional love can help enhance the sexual experience by creating a safe space free from judgment and expectations. This can allow you both to feel comfortable expressing your true desires, needs, and passions. It can help to create deeper intimacy and connection in the relationship. This powerful act will transcend the mundane. In this book, you will learn techniques to expand and deepen the orgasm experience, so you can connect with Divine Feminine energy.

Sex worship is what you are doing to worship your woman as she becomes a goddess. Sex worship becomes the ritual you will perform throughout your relationship to help your goddess achieve her transcendental cosmic orgasms. She will allow you to feel those orgasms with her. Your sex worship becomes a ceremony, a celebration of the Feminine Divine. You become more connected to your goddess and the Divine

Feminine power of creation in the universe when you bring your goddess to orgasm. Ceremonial sex worship is a practice of honoring the sexual energy between two partners and reverence for the feminine form. It is done as a ritual, in which your woman's inner goddess is invoked and connected with. It is a practice of expressing love and appreciation for the feminine energy and presence by creating an atmosphere of safety, intimacy, and trust.

CHAPTER 3

What Is the Divine Feminine?

To truly appreciate goddess power, it's important to understand Divine Feminine. The Divine Feminine is the feminine aspect of the divine power that connects and binds the Earth together. In other words, it is the goddess energy that exists within all of us. Many ancient cultures have a Divine Feminine concept. The Egyptians had Isis, the Greeks had Aphrodite, and the Hindus had Shakti. Aspects of the Divine Feminine can be found in almost all ancient and modern belief systems.

The Divine Feminine is often associated with fertility, creativity, and intuition. Everyone has both Divine Feminine and divine masculine qualities. The concept of "masculine" and "feminine" energy has been used in many different mystical practices throughout history to describe the dualities that exist within everyone. While the Divine Feminine represents the nurturer and healer within us, the masculine symbolizes the inherent leader. Divine means "supremely good," "heavenly," and "Godlike." Feminine can be described as the embodiment or conception of a timeless or idealized feminine nature. The Divine Feminine has several modern manifestations and a long religious history worldwide. Goddesses were worshipped extensively in older polytheistic religions and are heavily represented in Roman, Greek, African, and Egyptian contexts. In Hinduism, goddesses are still worshipped and Tantric Buddhism and Tantric Hinduism both have a specific focus on female deities.

The feminine and the masculine are not singular and separate energies—instead, they exist in balance. The two energies depend on one another. In Hindu, Shakti means power. According to goddess worship cult in Hinduism, in the beginning there was nothing except Shiva in the static form and Shakti in the kinetic form. Shakti invoked Shiva and thus the universe was born. Shiva is associated with matter and time, and Shakti is energy and space. Shakti is the World Mother. Her installation is done in human forms with distinctive features and characters and worshipped as goddesses.

All Hindu goddesses are referred to as Shakti in a single, consistent form, but sometimes more precisely to denote the consort of Shiva. Shakti is the Sanskrit word for energy. Goddess worship was very important in ancient times so it's no surprise that women were considered the vessels of Shakti and goddess power was related to the creation of the universe. It is female energy because females give birth; they create.

Men support the creation but ultimately it is the woman from whom new life emerges. In the same way that goddesses were worshipped so too must you, the submissive supportive gentleman, worship your goddess and help her to unleash and experience her power. Through your focus on the female orgasm and connecting to her divine center, you facilitate the connection to the divine and you both experience her goddess power.

The Divine Feminine was considered sacred and was worshipped as the matrix of creation. In many ancient societies, the nurturing nature of the Divine Feminine was associated with the concepts of fertility and creation and took the shape of the Great Mother Goddess. We find the goddess religion in many parts of the ancient world long before patriarchal religions took over. Societies were structured and operated around these goddess religions and were ruled by a collective of priestesses who were devoted to ritual.

Women had a significant role and acted as priestesses and possibly religious leaders. For the most part, these societies were matriarchal and developed peaceful cultures, with no fortification up until the appearance of the warrior societies. The Mother Goddess, often known as Mother Earth, is a matriarchal archetype represented frequently in ancient art and found in various mythologies around the world.

For our ancestors, the embodiment of the Divine Feminine was the Earth itself. The ancients, who had more direct contact and a greater relationship with nature, viewed the Earth as this gigantic female being who gives birth and continuously creates life. They observed and witnessed the plants and animals being born on the Earth's surface, multiplying and finally returning to her, only to come back again through regeneration. A cycle that is maintained steadfast: birth, death, and rebirth. Earth supports the whole ecosystem, the sky, mountains, trees, seas and rivers, animals, and humans; she nurtures and heals all.

Ultimately all life depends on her; she is the force of creation and destruction. Our ancients did not take this for granted but saw all of these as blessed gifts and therefore considered themselves as children of the Earth. Earth was the divine mother of all.

The first written reference to the Earth as a mother is traced back to ancient Greek writings. Gaia was the great goddess and mother of all creation for the ancient Greeks. The concept of Mother Earth or Mother Goddess was first recorded in the early 7th century BCE by the great Greek poet Hesiod in his poem "Theogony." Hesiod records the story of the birth of the universe, when in the beginning it was only Chaos, Gaia, and Eros. The Earth was therefore a primal deity; she was revered as the mother of all gods and living creatures and symbolized the rejuvenating care of Mother Nature.

Growth as a goddess celebrates a feminine energy in that we give life to something that was not there before. Archetypes of femininity and fertility from around the world and throughout history are abundant, and exploration of the Divine Feminine takes on many historical, anthropological, spiritual, and cultural forms. The Divine Feminine restores a balance to your goddess worship. Just as the Earth must be in balance, we must also be balanced. Many women are experiencing their personal awakening. Women have been disenfranchised for thousands of years. Feminine energy has been given very little respect, and we have all lost out as a result.

Women now make up 47 percent of the U.S. workforce. They are demanding equal pay and are currently more likely than men to have a college degree. This is tangible evidence of the rise of the female voice using her energy, courage, and power. Hence the rise of Female Led Relationships as well. More than perhaps ever before, right now is a divine time to help your Queen connect to her inner feminine energy — otherwise known as the Divine Feminine. The world desperately needs more compassion, empathy, and warmth, which are the natural skills and intentions of divine femininity. You connect to your Queen's divine center when you worship her sexually and you help her to unleash her sex goddess. Your Queen must be encouraged to explore her own desire to become a true Goddess of Love.

It is important for you to recognize how much you really love her feminine energy. How much you love what makes your Queen beautiful, with her capacity to love, her laughter, her freedom to feel and express emotion. You must discover and then learn to worship the feminine face of your divine goddess. A goddess's purpose isn't to own people, rule them, manipulate them, or instruct them. Her only purpose is to live her own truth and meet her own desires, and in achieving that single-minded focus on her own pleasures, she lifts others up by being an example to those who want the same. Men are absolutely turned on by her because she can have any man she wants.

A goddess chooses the man who will serve her. It isn't for society nor culture to define what a good man is, it is for her to decide who will please her now. The most powerful women in the world do not need men for anything other than their own pleasure. When a woman has reached that level of self-possession, self-assurance, independence, supreme confidence in her own being, she has awakened the goddess within. At this point, she lives life for her own pleasure, and she alone decides who she will take pleasure in.

A goddess bestows her energy on men who worship her properly, and those blessings amount to superhuman confidence, life's purpose, inner drive, and sharp focus on attaining their goals, their spiritual and earthly wealth. Through her, they receive their power to succeed, something all men crave, and will do anything for her. She needs nothing from them, just like the great God in heaven needs nothing from you. She simply delights in what she receives.

When worshipped to her full satisfaction, to the point when she lives in a state of permanent orgasm, nirvana, and bliss, your goddess will bless you, the man in her life with power. This is why in ancient times, and in the present, the most powerful men on Earth still take part in goddess worship.

A goddess generates her own energy, her own power. She shares that positive energy with all. She does not take energy from others. Ever. To clarify, incomplete human beings need the energy of others to survive. They seek attention and look for their purpose in others. Goddesses radiate pure, positive energy at all times. They need nothing to thrive.

Men are attracted to women because of their Divine Feminine energy. This is due to the influence and power of sexual polarity. Polarity essentially means opposites. In terms of attraction, this means that the Divine Feminine is attracted to the divine masculine, and vice versa. A Queen embodying the sacred feminine will be operating from her feminine power. This makes her very attracted to a man with strong male energy. The feminine is the Mother. She is the creator, giver, and bearer of life. The feminine is the caregiver, the maternal figure who loves unconditionally and wholeheartedly. A feminine woman is dynamic, flowing, and always moving. This woman said to be in her feminine is in a state of flow. Feminine energy is no less powerful. We think of the power of Mother Nature and the impacts we have witnessed on Earth.

Both men and women have masculine and feminine energy within them. Masculine energy traits are: presence, confidence, logic, ration, security, honesty, trustworthiness, reliability, achieving, dominant. Feminine energy traits are: dynamic, flowing, receptive, open, intuitive, trusting, creative, passive, authentic, caring, vulnerable, and supportive.

A strong Queen can help you to balance both sides of this energy. Hence, they create a more harmonious existence in your Female Led Relationship or marriage. The female orgasm is the focus of goddess worship. However, both yours and your Queen's orgasms are necessary as the connection and energy exchange between both partners is essential when it comes to honoring the Divine Feminine. The focus is on embracing pleasure and connection as this is what helps create a powerful, spiritual experience. You should learn to experience most of your euphoria from your goddess's pleasure. In Tantric sex, the male energy is like fire—burning hot and fast, but a woman's energy is like water, it flows like a river.

When you honor your goddess through worship, you enable the Divine Feminine. Honoring your spiritual connection is the most powerful way to be connected. I feel that today, this is the missing link. The spiritual connection is a pathway to happiness. Your goddess is your pathway to the universe, Divine Feminine, and the goddess that lies within women. As partners in a union, the responsibility is on you and your Queen to create the happiness you are seeking through the daily female led communication, worship, rituals, affirmations, and daily services you perform in your Female Led Relationship. This is what makes female led life so special.

Mother Earth represents the feminine energy of the universe. The energy of life is the greatest energy of the universe. When you unleash the feminine energy of life in your goddess, you open up pathways to improve your lives exponentially because both male and female energy are released.

Unlike traditional intercourse, where the male focus is on physical pleasure, sexual worship focuses on harnessing feminine energy, empowering your goddess, and bringing new vitality to your female led life. This can only happen through the worship of the woman through oral and penetrative sex worship when it is performed as a focus and prolonged experience for the goddess's pleasure. This transcendental sexual worship takes both of you to a higher spiritual level. Goddesses swear by the power of sexual energy. If sexual energy can create human life, it can certainly help to manifest other great things in your life. This spiritual sexual energy is the energy derived from the Divine Feminine and has a greater connection with the divine or the spiritual universe than the physical world.

Sexual energy can also have healing and transformative properties, which can be used to promote spiritual and emotional healing, as well as help people in their spiritual journey to find meaning and purpose in life. It is the view of sex as just physical movements which leads to the breakdown of the spiritual side of sex worship and its connection with the

Divine Feminine energy of the universe, which is the source of the overall breakdown of many relationships. As the main supporter and servant to your queen, the responsibility falls on your shoulders to transfer sex into sex worship and empower your woman to become a goddess. You will need to create the right worship experiences in which you will use and harness Divine Feminine sexual energy to create the highest level Female Led Relationship.

Why is it the gentleman's responsibility? By nature, gentlemen are much more aggressive about sex. So instead of focusing on the physical sex worship act, which lasts a few minutes and largely leaves the goddess unsatisfied, you can now create a spiritual sexual worship experience for your goddess that fulfills her on a physical, mental, and spiritual level and helps her unleash her inner sex goddess and connect to the Divine Feminine.

Feminine energy is centered around values such as love, kindness, and partnership. Contrastingly, masculine energy values organization, structure, routine, achievement, and rigidity. Both need to be cultivated daily. The power of merging the two is that when there is a polarity between two people, we experience the meeting of both yin and yang energies. There is mutual cooperation and balance. Deep sexual intimacy is abundant. Sexual chemistry flows. Lovemaking is intensely passionate, steamy, and wild. This is what I believe helps your Queen to unleash her sex goddess and become a Goddess of Love.

Inside a relationship, when feminine energy is balanced with masculine energy, there is harmony. There is flow, smoothness, and intense attraction. You want your Queen to be balanced and able to step into her goddess power through the Divine Feminine.

If you are blessed enough to be a gentleman who a goddess bestows her energy onto, you must be able to properly worship her. Being with a goddess will allow a man to experience countless blessings as they share in the goddess's superhuman confidence, life's purpose, inner drive, sharp goal-oriented focus, and her accumulation of earthly and spiritual wealth.

Through her, a man can receive the power to succeed, either in society or as her stay-at-home submissive gentleman. She needs nothing from men, and she simply delights in the love, obedience, service, and worship she receives from them. When worshipped to her full satisfaction, a goddess lives in a state of permanent orgasmic-Nirvana and bliss. In return for your devotion, your goddess will bless you with her Divine Feminine energy. This is why in ancient times, and in the present, the most powerful gentlemen on Earth have taken and will take part in goddess worship.

A goddess draws her own energy and power from the Divine Feminine energy, which is boundless. She shares some of this powerful energy with her submissive man. She does not take energy from her sub, rather she gives it to her sub. Incomplete submissive men need the energy of a woman or a goddess to survive. They seek attention and look for their purpose in their woman or goddess. Women who become goddesses radiate pure, positive energy at all times. They need no man to thrive. Men are actually attracted to women because of their Divine Feminine energy. This is due to the influence and power of sexual polarity, which is essential to romantic relationships and is defined as the different energies that draw two people together. Both energies are necessary for a relationship to be balanced.

In terms of attraction, this means that the Divine Feminine is attracted to the divine masculine, and vice versa. A woman embodying the sacred feminine will be operating from her full feminine power. This makes her very attractive to a gentleman and is why many submissive gentlemen can be "alpha males" with strong male energy.

As stated, the feminine is the mother and is the creator, giver, and bearer of life. The feminine is the caregiver, the maternal figure who loves unconditionally and wholeheartedly. But always remember the power of Mother Nature; hurricanes, floods, earthquakes, and other natural disasters, and you can see why you don't mess with Mother Nature nor your goddess. So be a good submissive gentleman.

As a strong woman transforms into a Goddess of Love, she will help you balance both sides of your energy. Hence, an FLR woman will create a more harmonious existence in your relationship. Feminine energy is centered around values such as love, kindness, and partnership.

Contrastingly, masculine energy values organization, structure, routine, achievement, and rigidity. The power of merging the two energies is when we experience the meeting of both yin and yang energies. There is mutual cooperation and balance. Deep sexual intimacy is abundant. Sexual chemistry flows. Sexual worship is intensely passionate, steamy, and energetic. This is what I believe helps your woman unleash her inner goddess and become a Goddess of Love. When Divine Feminine energy leads and balances with masculine energy, there is harmony, flow, and intense attraction. In this balanced FLR, the woman can complete her journey to become a Goddess of Love, powering your relationship with her Divine Feminine energy.

CHAPTER 4

What Is a Goddess of Love?

A Female Led Relationship encourages a gentleman to worship his Queen. She is an extraordinary woman who is a great leader and she has the ability to become a Goddess of Love. Men seek beauty because it is often seen as a reflection of a female's inner health, happiness, and vitality. Men are also attracted to physical beauty because it is seen to be a sign of the "Mother Earth Life Force" or good genetic material and is associated with fertility and the ability to create life. Beauty is often seen as a sign of health, youthfulness, and femininity, which are all attractive qualities in humans.

As her submissive gentleman, it is your job is to support your woman through her evolution to becoming a Goddess of Love. Submissive gentlemen serve a goddess in life by living according to the rules outlines in all 14 of my books in my Female Led Relationship series. By helping your Queen to make the ultimate transformation to become a Goddess of Love, you give her the greatest gift she could ever receive in life. You do this through your goddess worship sessions, respect, reinforcing her supremacy and leadership in your life, making sure she is properly sexually satisfied, obeying her commands, and celebrating her connection to the divine. Just as a priest helps people connect to God, your duty is to help your Queen with her transition into goddess life.

The Female Led Relationship is how you achieve this paradigm shift in life. What do couples in an FLR do differently? They have different values, beliefs, and practices when compared to patriarchal couples. The gentlemen have a deep personal relationship with their women, which consists of trusting her and holding her rules as their source for guidance on how to live their lives. FLR couples should have strong convictions about the spiritual aspects of their sexuality and find their sense of purpose in serving their goddess and her Queendom.

Male led couples, on the other hand, may find their sense of purpose and morality from other sources, such as science, humanism, or secularism. They may be skeptical of the spirituality of the goddess and a woman's connection to the Divine Feminine. Men often are more self-centered and women must yield to their wants and desires. It's completely opposite of a female led life where a gentleman has a higher purpose in not only exploring his own evolution but learning to be of service to the most important person in his life—his Queen and goddess. Your Queen as a Goddess of Love understands the spiritual side of life and how to merge the sexual with the spiritual. A spiritual sexual life is a way of living in which a gentleman seeks to deepen his connection with the higher power or divine energy of his goddess and therefore elevate himself. This includes many FLR practices and engaging in mindfulness or spiritual thoughts while engaged in the sexual worship of the goddess.

When your Queen is one with her inner Goddess of Love, she experiences so many benefits. She is not only seeking pleasure but is engaging in a spiritual sexual connection to the Divine Feminine energy of the universe and your overall well-being as a couple. You and your goddess are more likely to find more love and intimacy in an FLR. This female focus ultimately improves your goddess's ability to express how she wants to be worshipped during your relationship. What sets a Goddess of Love apart is their ability to let go and enjoy sex. Men love to see their women enjoying themselves and being in the moment, but you must help your woman unleash her inner Goddess of Love flow.

A woman who wants to be a Goddess of Love is open-minded and confident enough to explore all aspects of sex and communicate her fantasies, desires, likes, and dislikes to you, her submissive gentleman. You must encourage the exploration of all of her fantasies together and use each day as an opportunity to bolster her confidence and encourage her to be free to engage in "sexploration" with you. The more you lift up your woman and support her evolution into becoming a Goddess of Love, the more every experience is going to bring you closer to each other. A Goddess of Love is free to be themselves during sex worship. They're open to new positions, toys, techniques, and alternative lifestyles. She'll genuinely enjoy all aspects of sex worship and, in turn, you both will experience a transformation in your daily life with a very sex-worship-goddess vibe.

A woman or a Goddess of Love in an FLR experiences the opposite. In a female led life, everything is female-focused, including sex. Learning how to be a Goddess of Love enables your Queen to meet her needs without external validation and consciously communicate her desires to receive maximum sexual satisfaction during all forms of worship. Being a Goddess of Love can help women express who they truly are and what they're about. The quest to release your woman's inner Goddess of Love gives her the confidence to surrender to the rhythm of her sexual desires and this, ultimately, extends into other areas of Life.

Sex is not a mystery. Sex becomes an essential part of FLR, and changing the dialogue surrounding female sexuality is essential. The goddess movement includes spiritual beliefs or practices which emerged predominantly in North America, Western Europe, Australia, and New Zealand in the 1970s. The movement grew as a reaction to perceptions of predominant organized religion as patriarchal in nature and male-dominated. The *Love and Obey* Female Led Relationship Movement makes use of goddess worship because it centers the focus on women and supporting their goals and dreams. Goddess worship becomes your life purpose and only when you commit to this mission does your relationship completely evolve into the highest level of female pleasure, intimacy, connection, and bond with her male submissive. It is through real goddess worship that you will help your woman to achieve the next level status of Goddess of Love.

One of the greatest gifts you can give your Queen is to help her unlock her inner sex goddess. She must learn how to harness the power of her femininity, nurture her authentic self, and discover what brings her joy and fulfillment, which can develop self-awareness and cultivate emotional intelligence. You and your Queen need to practice self-care and create healthy boundaries. By fully embracing her goddess nature, she can become more confident and lead a happier and more fulfilled life. You also reap the benefits of a happier, sexier Queen who is more exciting and vibrant.

Women need the power of the divine in their lives and they unleash their inner goddess by tapping into their power and discovering their own unique gifts and purpose. Your Queen must learn to honor and celebrate her intuition, feelings, and desires. Surrounding yourselves with positivity and utilizing the affirmations (stated in Chapter 20) in your lovemaking is a great way to focus on goddess worship and supporting your Queen during her transformation.

The more time you both devote to the practice of your spirituality, the faster you will see results. I believe that one of the most important steps in a relationship is to deepen your spiritual connection by incorporating worship into all aspects of your life. The more you worship your Goddess of Love and encourage her to explore these deeper areas of her life, the more intimacy you create and the more you witness a transformation in your own life as her main supporter. Men have an incredibly important role to play in a Queen's transformation, and together you both create a dream life.

The first step for your Queen to become a Goddess of Love is by getting to know who she is and her unique strengths, interests, and passions. Once she has identified those areas, she needs to take the time to explore different activities and experiences to further understand herself. Maybe you will join her in a class on meditation or yoga, or perhaps you will take her dancing or take time to be together. The exploration can still be done together with your encouragement. You reinforce her discovery of her inner goddess by referring to her as "my Queen" and "my goddess" in all of your communication. Constant daily reinforcement is what helps her to accept and step into her role as a goddess. She will begin to reflect and think about her role as a goddess and her connection to the Divine Feminine each and every day.

I have personally witnessed changes in women in a few weeks of doing this daily practice. Queens who never believed in goddess power are openly embracing their inner sex goddess and it's dramatically transforming their lives and their Female Led Relationships. You both should take time to reflect on your dreams, aspirations, and values to determine what truly brings you joy and fulfillment. Set aside time each day to reflect on your goals and objectives. Think about what it is that you ultimately want to achieve and what your life purpose is.

Also, try to remain mindful of your thoughts, feelings, and behaviors, as they can tell you a lot about who you really are. Take time to develop your passions and interests. Explore new activities together and take steps toward learning more about what truly brings you fulfillment and make improvements as necessary. The idea is your life becomes a journey of exploration and goddess worship enriches what is already a foundation of your Female Led Relationship.

As she transitions into becoming a goddess, your Queen can cultivate emotional intelligence by developing self-awareness and understanding of her emotions. This can include taking time to reflect on her experiences, thoughts, and feelings in order to gain insight into how she processes her emotions. She must develop empathy and the ability to recognize the emotions of others, which can help her to cultivate emotional intelligence. She should practice active listening and open dialogue with those around her.

Mindfulness practice can help her focus on the present moment and ensure she is present and engaged in her interactions. Finally, you and your Queen must develop effective communication skills which allow both of you to express your feelings and create a healthier relationship.

Practicing self-care is also extremely important. Investing in your own well-being, by engaging in activities that support and nurture your physical, spiritual, and emotional well-being, is crucial. Examples of self-care activities include getting enough sleep, engaging in a regular exercise routine, spending time in nature, eating nutritious meals, taking time for quiet reflection and meditation, practicing gratitude, and doing something creative and enjoyable.

Next, it's important for you and your goddess to create healthy boundaries. Respect each other's limits. Goddess nature is the intuitive, sacred, and divinely feminine energies that exist within each woman. One way for your Queen to connect to her goddess nature is to spend time surrounded by nature, take time to make space for meditation and contemplation, listen to her heart and follow its guidance, create art and rituals that are meaningful to you, spend time alone, practice yoga and mindful movement, and connect to the energies of your body and the Divine Feminine. Spend time getting to know her and what makes her feel beautiful, powerful, and whole.

In general, here are some life tips and advice you can help your goddess to tap into her inner goddess powers:

- Your Queen can greatly benefit from seeking out female role models and mentors who have achieved success in areas that inspire her. Some of the most famous female role models for tapping into one's inner goddess powers are Oprah Winfrey, Malala Yousafzai, Michelle Obama, Ruth Bader Ginsburg, Gloria Steinem, Maya Angelou, and Angela Davis.

- Rediscover her passions, interests, and pursuits that excite and motivate her. Maybe she loves art or movies, or she enjoys a sport or being outdoors. Perhaps your Queen loved dancing or theater. It's important for both of you to engage in her passions.

- Your Queen needs to visualize her ideal self and the life she wants to live. She needs to visualize her ideal self and the life she deserves by setting goals, reflecting on what she is passionate about, and creating a step-by-step plan to reach her goals. You both can use the power of affirmations as I outlined in my book *Turning Point*.

- You both need to celebrate your successes and honor your femininity. Your Queen can celebrate her success and honor her femininity by spending time with family and friends, engaging in activities that make her happy, engaging in self-care, expressing gratitude for what she has accomplished, and allowing herself to take a break and rest. She can also celebrate her femininity by embracing her unique qualities and using her voice to speak up for herself and make a positive impact in the world.

- Your Queen needs to be aligned with her emotional intelligence by learning how to recognize, understand, and express her emotions. She can also develop tools to practice self-care, identify her triggers and what sets off her emotions, and learn to respond to situations in a thoughtful and mindful way. Taking time for self-reflection and gaining insight into her patterns of behavior can also help unlock her inner goddess and live more confidently.

- You can help your Queen live her most joyful and satisfying life. A woman can live her most joyful and satisfying life by connecting with her inner goddess. Through cultivating emotional intelligence, self-care, and mindfulness, she can tap into her inner wisdom and develop self-confidence to reach her goals and follow her passions. Living as a goddess means living life to its fullest, embracing her unique qualities, and taking steps to make a positive impact in the world.

As her supportive submissive gentleman, you play an important role in supporting your Queen as she unlocks her inner goddess. You must be a kind and nonjudgmental listener for her as she explores her connection to her Divine Feminine, offering compassionate and loving guidance. You can also offer his unconditional support, respect, and love when she embarks on this spiritual journey and self-exploration. You can help her to create her own sacred space where she can feel safe expressing unique and authentic aspects of herself. Finally, you can foster an environment of appreciation, admiration, and deepening connection between each other, as you both learn and grow together.

The best way for you both to begin a journey of transforming your Queen into a goddess is to start by talking openly and honestly about each other's desires and expectations. Setting boundaries and communication can help create a safe and comfortable space in which each person can feel secure to explore and expand. Establishing mutual respect and appreciation for each other can help strengthen trust. Additionally, engaging in activities such as sexual worship, yoga, meditation, and using goddess female led affirmations can help cultivate feelings of mindfulness and self-awareness, allowing a couple to deepen their connection and explore desires with intention.

You both can tap into the Divine Feminine together through mindful activities and be respectful of each other's boundaries. You can cultivate feelings of reverence and love, honoring different aspects of femininity such as intuition, sensuality, nurturing, and creativity. Activities can include engaging in sacred rituals and ceremonies, doing bodywork such as massage or Reiki, or creating yoga and meditation practices together. Other activities can include sharing sacred stories, dancing and movement, listening to music, creating art, and exploring one's sexuality. Creating an intentional space dedicated to connecting with the Divine Feminine can help to deepen the connection between the couple while furthering the individual's own journey of unlocking the inner goddess.

As her submissive man, you can worship your Queen after she has discovered her inner goddess by nurturing her and celebrating her Divine Feminine energy. You should express your appreciation and love for her through words and touch, respecting her journey. You can also support and honor her own processes of spiritual growth and creativity. You can invest in activities such as creating sacred spaces, sharing meaningful moments, exploring sexuality, and connecting with nature. Above all, you will need to be patient and mindful of her needs and desires, cultivating love and trust with intention, and being committed to honoring her autonomy and self-expression.

You can show respect to your Queen by listening to her and acknowledging her feelings and thoughts. You should always show her compassion and empathy, being supportive in both the small and big moments. You can express your love and appreciation through words, touch, and gestures. You should take time to build trust with her, encouraging her to make her own choices and celebrating her successes. Additionally, create a safe space where she can express herself, exploring her spiritual growth and creativity without fear or judgment. Finally, you must always respect her autonomy, honoring her boundaries and decisions.

In a Female Led Relationship, you are submissive to your Queen, and you encourage her to lead, so you need to give her the space to make decisions and offer support when needed. You should be understanding and accepting of her opinions, even if they conflict with your own, and be willing to compromise if necessary. Additionally, you should practice active listening, asking questions, and allowing her to fully explain her position. You should always honor her autonomy, encouraging her to trust her instincts and not forcing her into anything she doesn't feel comfortable with. Ultimately, you should strive to create an atmosphere of mutual respect and understanding to ensure the relationship is built on trust and respect.

You must be open to allowing your Queen to lead. Supporting her ideas, feelings, and actions will show a profound level of respect for her and foster trust based on mutual support. This type of dynamic has the potential to create an atmosphere of love and understanding, which in turn can bring forth and strengthen a Divine Feminine energy that empowers the relationship. These are some areas you can focus on:

- **Demonstrate Respect.** Showing respect for your Queen can be a powerful way to demonstrate your submission. Allow her to feel safe and valued by validating her feelings, respecting her boundaries, and being an active listener.

- **Embrace Your Vulnerability**. Allow yourself to embrace your vulnerability with your Queen. Opening up to her will allow you both to grow closer and make the relationship stronger by building trust and transparency. Remember, it is okay if you are still struggling to make the full transition to accepting female superiority. It's your journey.

- **Acknowledge your Queen's authority.** Acknowledge your Queen's authority and her decisions, allowing her to lead while offering your support. This will show that you trust her and are comfortable with her leading and empowering you.

When you are submissive to your Queen who has unlocked her inner goddess, the relationship flows better because it creates a healthy balance of power dynamic. It enables both of you to feel equally respected and valued, which fosters a more intimate and trusting connection. You feel more secure in the relationship and you know that your Queen has the strength and stability to lead. With an inner goddess, she can better learn to accept and express the power that is rightfully theirs. Achieving this balance builds a strong foundation of trust, understanding, and connection, ultimately making the relationship more pleasurable and fulfilling.

When a woman with an unlocked inner goddess takes control and leads, relationships work better because she has the confidence and ability to provide a steady and empowered direction for the relationship. This encourages communication, trust, and mutual respect, which are all key components in a successful relationship. She can exercise her creative and intuitive abilities, making each partnership unique and special. The Queen can effectively take charge of the relationship without compromising her partner's autonomy or peace of mind, allowing both individuals to feel comfortable and secure in the relationship. This combination of confidence and collaboration helps create balance and harmony between partners, a foundation for a strong, healthy, and fulfilling relationship.

When your Queen embodies her inner goddess and leads her relationship with the strength, confidence, and creative spirit of the Divine Feminine energy, the relationships can become empowered by those qualities. The goddess-like leadership creates balance, harmony, and growth within the partnership, allowing trust, understanding, and mutual respect to blossom. This is because Divine Feminine energy is based on connection, loving communication, and collaboration—meaning that through leading with this energy, relationships can become more powerful.

When your Queen becomes empowered as a sex goddess, it gives her the confidence to lead and use her intuition, especially throughout your relationship. This allows her to have better self-expression and to better understand her own feelings and needs. It also makes her more powerful because she can use her power to bring about positive change in her relationships as well as within herself.

Men love it when they are able to submit to and follow a Queen who has fully embraced their inner goddess. It gives them a sense of reverence and admiration for their partner as they find strength, support, and guidance in her. Men may seek to submit to a goddess because they trust her judgment and decisions and also admire her Divine power and beauty. Ultimately, men seek the ability to give in to a goddess's authority because they thrive when they are given permission to surrender and explore deeper, spiritual, supportive, and committed love. Men experience more intimacy and connection than ever before, and I believe they actually crave this in their lives.

Men want to submit to a beautiful strong woman who is a goddess because they may find power and strength attractive in a Queen. They may be drawn to the idea of being with a woman who is emotionally and intellectually mature, has a strong sense of self, and has goals she is committed to. Men may also see a powerful woman as a challenge and desire the mental and emotional connection that comes from submitting to her authority.

It is important for you to view your Queen not just as a romantic partner, but as a goddess and spiritual guide who can help to navigate your life. By submitting to your Queen and allowing her to take the lead in certain aspects of your relationship, you can develop a reverence and admiration for the power and grace of a goddess. You can also look at a woman's inner beauty and wisdom, and learn to appreciate her strong, capable, and compassionate nature. When you take the time to really appreciate all that she offers, it can lead to a deep reverence and admiration for her. This in itself takes your Female Led Relationship and female led marriage to a whole new level.

By submitting to your goddess, you allow her to step into her power and demonstrate her strength, leadership, and wisdom. Women have always been taught to allow men to be in charge, so even though they are capable of leadership, they need to be encouraged and supported to take the lead. For a relationship to work better, open communication is key, as each person must be willing to compromise and make decisions together. Respect must be mutual, trust must be established and maintained, and commitment should be present as both partners are committing to each other. Allowing for individuality and providing mutual support can also strengthen the relationship. In essence, a successful relationship relies on a strong foundation of communication, respect, trust, and commitment from both partners.

Men may find feminine power and strength attractive because it indicates confidence, strength of character, and an openness to growth. Feminine power and strength can also indicate a secure and complicated inner life, as well as a willingness to take risks and stand up for what she believes in. Ultimately, it is an individual choice and experience, and no two people will experience it the same way.

CHAPTER 5

Goddess Traditions

G oddess worship begins with an understanding of the traditions. Goddess traditions around the world have guided people through the most important phases in the human life cycle—birth, sexual initiation, procreation, disease and death, and the prospect of rebirth. They provide answers to perennial questions about the meaning of life, our place within the cosmos, and our relationship to the Source of all being and becoming. Goddess traditions give divine meaning and inspiration to key life experiences.

Every woman is a goddess. All women have the power to not only bring life to Earth but also possess an intimate connection to nature, the elements of fire, Earth, air, and water, as well as, to the realms of magic itself. Before patriarchy took over the world, all civilizations were goddess-centric matriarchies that were in harmony with the forces of the heavens above and the Earth.

The goddess and goddess worship can be traced back to the Paleolithic and Neolithic ages. The development of the religion of the female deity in this area was intertwined with the earliest beginnings of religion. At one time, the goddess was unquestionably the supreme deity, creator of the universe, prophetess, provider of human destinies, inventor, healer, hunter, and leader. This makes sense because the creation of life really begins in a woman's belly.

Generally, goddesses provide archetypal energies and role models for women and girls, while Gods and priests provide archetypal energies and role models for men and boys. However, evidence shows that goddesses sometimes presided over whole cities and civilizations and were worshipped as the primary deity by men and women, for example, in Greece, Europe, India, Japan, Hawaii, Brazil, and numerous North American Native Indian tribes.

For much of human history, people believed they were created by deities and so invoked their powers and gifts through religious rites. Goddess spirituality is the reverential experiencing and expressing of Divine Feminine energies within the universe. It offers these benefits through the prism of Divine Feminine energies, energies of the cosmos. Goddess spirituality can be understood psychologically in the concepts of conscious and unconscious gestalts that result from personal experience, family inter-relationships, and transpersonal constellations of behaviors as mother, father, daughter, son, spouse, lover, healer, oracle, wise elder, etc. Archetypal energies may have been repressed from conscious memory but remain encoded in psycho-spiritual patterns, having profound influences on the choices of one's day-to-day life.

There has been a tremendous resurgence today of goddess spirituality, which has grown in tandem with the worldwide women's liberation movement. Both seek to get rid of over-masculinization of cultures and associated fundamentalist patriarchal religions and change patriarchal ways of life. I believe this has tremendous benefit to modern Female Led Relationships, as once a woman embodies her goddess power, she and her supportive gentleman can transform her household and have a positive effect on many others. We can learn a great deal from goddess traditions and incorporate it into our lives.

Why Is Goddess Worship Beneficial?

Queens are turned on by men who bow down to a goddess. Why? The more you worship goddesses, the more you develop and respect the Divine Feminine. Grace, compassion, empathy, care, concern, and sensitivity, all flow from the Divine Feminine. Submissive supportive gentlemen are never considered weak or inconsequential when they serve their Queen and help her to become a goddess. Some of the bravest warriors have used the power of goddesses on the battlefield, vying to earn their blessings for victory against the enemy. There is a reason why armies went out to fight for their Queen.

You must acknowledge the human embodiment and expression of Divine Feminine energy in your Queen, which flows through all females. You are helping to reclaim a Queen's place as goddess by learning to worship the Divine Feminine.

Minoan Culture and Treating Women as Equals

One of the first cultures to treat women as equals was in the Minoan Crete. It was considered the center of the Bronze

Age trading system. The people of ancient Crete followed the megalithic tradition. Women and men had equal rights. Wall paintings from the palaces of Knossos and Phaistos show that women were able to express themselves freely. Statues, vases, and wall paintings show images of sporting contests where women competed equally alongside men. The island's favorite sport was the impossible-sounding bull-vaulting. An acrobat (sometimes female) would grab the horns of a bull and somersault onto its back. Then, in a second somersault, she would leap off its back and land upright, with her feet back on the ground.

Women did not dominate society, but they did oversee it. Frescoes at the palace of Thera, on the island of Santorini, north of Crete, show women standing on balconies overseeing processions of young men carrying an animal for sacrifice. Most priests on Minoan Crete were female. In Minoan law, women retained full control of their property. They even had the right to divorce at pleasure. They could freely choose any man they desired. They seemed to be the first examples of a female led society.

CHAPTER 6

What is Tantric Sex?

To learn about goddess worship and to help your Queen become a sex goddess, you should have an understanding of Tantra and Tantric sex. Tantra is an ancient Indian practice that has a presence today around the world. Imagine, 5,000 years ago, this practice being developed, explored, and enhanced to promote sexuality, spirituality, and emotional interconnectedness. Tantra honors and celebrates our bodies and enriches sensual pleasure, not just sexual pleasure. Breath, meditation, mindfulness, movement, and our environment can enhance intimacy with oneself and others.

The word Tantra has many meanings, including "the way," "transformation," and "expansion through awareness."

Tantra involves unlocking the inner divine, which is defined as everything your body has to offer in terms of sexual pleasure, orgasm, and holistic fulfillment in general. Mantras have a lot of power when meditated upon and can be integrated into every aspect of your life.

Tantra mantra is the active, ritualistic meditation on the seven chakras. The most powerful mantra is widely recognized as the Gayatri mantra, which is an activation of the seventh crown chakra.

Tantra mantra works by channeling all chakras toward the seventh: to facilitate an understanding of each other that goes beyond a physical connection. Core principles are mindfulness and creativity.

Tantric techniques clear away the things that keep us from actualizing ourselves by channeling these energies. Embrace the present and let go of the past.

In Tantric sex, the breath and body awareness inherent in this principle is great for heightening both pleasure and intimacy. Opening the heart to connecting deeply with your Queen is an acceptance of love. When used in Tantric sex, it becomes a practice for radical self-acceptance as well as the acceptance of your Queen and goddess for who she is in the here and now.

Tantric love is the unity or interplay of masculine and feminine aspects. This principle encourages us to embrace both of these aspects within ourselves as well as within another person.

The masculine aspect is concerned with doing and achieving something within the mold of logic and reason; while the feminine aspect is all about being, the power of receiving, and being intuitive.

Tantric sexuality is really about dissolving binaries altogether. A life and sex life that integrates these principles emphasize deep connection and intentionality in all things.

Kundalini

Fundamental force of energy is kundalini. Dimensions of life only come into existence when you take action and activate yourself.

You have natural kundalini, but to activate more, you transform your life only if you are ready for it. In terms of Female Led Relationship, you should ensure you have practiced and are aware of core principles. Embarking on a journey to unleash the Divine Feminine and kundalini can be a life-changing force.

When kundalini rises in your body, it is important to be ready to make the necessary changes in both of your lives. The goal of your Female Led Relationship or female led marriage is to enrich your lives and make things better. But this can only happen through dedicated practice.

You can manifest any kind of love and happiness you want in your relationship or marriage with a focus on these dimensions. All creation begins in our minds, so you and your Queen must spend time working on what you want to manifest and create together. Assisting your Queen with becoming a Goddess of Love is only beneficial for both of you because she becomes a greater leader, and you are happier to serve a great Queen. She can direct your life better, and you both will have fewer arguments, less division, and more connection.

Anything you manifest in your life begins with your thoughts. When your mind is still, established, and directed, then everything in your body, mind, and spirit becomes more aligned, which transfers out into your daily interactions, friendships, relationships, and marriage. Everything around you and your Queen is affected by your thoughts and whatever you manifest in your FLR becomes with both of you and your connection. If your goals and needs are not aligned then there will always be destructive forces. As a Goddess of Love, your Queen is the most important person in your life because she is the director. So, you must do everything in your ability to empower the divine aspects of her. Of course, your evolution will be done together and the more bonded you are, the more happiness you will manifest in your lives.

Once you focus on preventing your mind from moving from a compulsive and obsessive state to a more conscious state, then you begin to see real changes in your relationship. Every decision and action you and your Queen take becomes much more conducive to affecting a positive change rather than negative.

Every day you wake up and spend your life force on empowering your Queen, providing inspiration, improving your connection to her, serving her, and attending to her deepest needs and vice versa, the more you are investing in real change and transformation. Your life has more meaning, more depth, and more fulfillment. How much thought do you actually spend on your relationship marriage? We know that we spend a lot of time thinking about stress, work, money, responsibilities, but how much thought is placed on the happiness you want to build with your Queen? This is the change you make when you inspire your Queen to become a Goddess of Love. You are spending more time on your thoughts about your relationship or marriage and what you both want out of it. This is how you use divine energy and kundalini to make a life-changing transformation. "It is not death that man must fear but never beginning to live," Marcus Aurelius once said.

Kundalini Sex and Cosmic Orgasm

As we have learned, kundalini refers to the source of all energy, the primal power. It is traditionally believed that the term comes from the Sanskrit Kundal, which literally means "coiled one" or from the word Kunda, meaning "deep place, cavity." It is often illustrated as a sleeping serpent coiled three and a half times. In all the oldest mystic traditions of the world, the serpent symbolizes consciousness. The three coils represent:

- Three Mantras of OM: past, present, and future

- Three Gunas, or states of consciousness: waking, sleeping, and dreaming

- Three types of experiences: subjective, sensual, and absence of experience

The half coil is the symbol of transcendence. Altogether, the coils express the total experience of the Universe.

In the human body, kundalini is situated at the root of the spine. In your Queen, it is located in the cervix, at the base of the uterus. Because of its seat at the root chakra, the kundalini powerhouse is expressed as sexual energy. Kundalini is the dormant potential force waiting to be awakened. In its first manifestation, the awakened energy is called Kali, the Hindu female goddess of death time and change. When you acquire mastery over your energy and are able to use it for beneficial purposes, there is the emergence of Durga, the higher and more refined symbol of the superconscious who bestows glory and beauty.

With the awakening of Kundalini, a metamorphosis takes place. You are no longer tapping into only a small percentage of your spiritual and sexual pleasure. You can experience a deep sense of joy and contentment that derives from being in full connection with your Queen's body and your soul. As if every cell in her body is shared with high voltage. You can come into contact with the Divine Power and recognize her Divine Nature.

The rise of kundalini energy triggers pleasure and power throughout your chakras. Both of you may experience a sense of enlightenment that makes you feel almost invincible. While the awakening may happen spontaneously, there are some practices that can trigger the process. In particular, breathing exercises and meditations can assist both of you in channeling your sexual energy.

There are two basic types of Tantric breathing:

1. Breathe through your nose slowly and rhythmically, as this breathing pattern is said to help you control your sexual energy. The slower and deeper you breathe through your nose, the more effective it is.

2. Breathe actively through your mouth. Managing this type of breathing can be beneficial to males who are about to orgasm during sex. They can exhale air more forcefully while tightening their abdomen. This provides more pleasure for themself and their partner.

Raising your kundalini energy can contribute much to your sexual and spiritual journey and will also get you and your Queen more connected and in touch with your potential for bliss. What you achieve during breathwork or sex is often called cosmic orgasm because it helps you both feel prolonged pleasure all over your body. The coiled snake that is your kundalini energy rises and slithers from your root chakra at the base up to your crown chakra at the top of the head. The process connects all your chakras, tapping at all the powers from each one, and then combining them for an explosive experience.

The Hindu traditions preach about the idea that absolute reality, while formless, also manifests itself as divine entities. So shakti, the formless source of everything, is understood to take on forms: goddesses, or personifications of the energies that make up the world and our consciousness. It helps you and your Queen become intimate with universal forces that otherwise can seem vast and impersonal. Paradoxically, goddess practice can also reveal how the forces that move our thoughts and emotions are ultimately not personal but are archetypal energies we all share.

Tantric Sex

The three major keys to moving energy in Tantra are breath, sound, and movement. Using these three keys, you can practice "running" your sexual energy throughout your body, whether you're engaged in sensual play or alone, and you can amp it up until it spills over into energetic orgasm. It can be such a profound and empowering aspect of connecting with your own innate sensuality. Steps to begin to get into the Tantric sex mood include getting prepared and creating the kind of space you'd like to be in to have any other kind of orgasm.

Foreplay can be anything you want it to be—oral, a massage, taking a shower together. But whatever you do, make sure you and your partner are fully present. Sit in front of your goddess. Look into each other's eyes. Move your bodies slightly as you breathe. After five minutes, touch each other sensually, taking turns massaging each other's arms, legs, neck, and other parts. After another five minutes, begin to kiss—and only kiss. Focus on every physical sensation you're feeling in the moment.

You both need to go within. Turn your attention inward, closing your eyes to signal to the mind that it's time to relax and let go. Open up your breath. Take some long, deep breaths to start, relaxing your entire body. Let the breath melt through any tension anywhere inside you. Then move into circular breathing, with no pause between the exhales or inhales. Connect to your sensuality. Focus your attention at the level of the genitals; connect to the quality of pleasure and eroticism within you. Fantasizing and caressing the whole body can help get you and your goddess get into the mood. Massage is vital to Tantric sex. You may perform your affirmations at any point before or during your session. Mix it up to keep your sex fresh and exciting.

Tantric sex involves sexual energy that goes beyond physical sensations of pleasure and genital orgasms. It is not limited to genital stimulation and the release of tension through a quick and simple orgasm. When spiritual sex is consciously practiced, there is a quality of "mindfulness," which is heightened awareness and expanded consciousness. The more cosmic experiences utilizing sexual energy create ecstatic states. The essence of Tantric sex is enhanced awareness, extraordinary inspiration, and a sense of merging with the life force.

What Tantric and spiritual experience of sex can do is increase conscious loving, which is sexual energy that generates intense, loving feelings for the partner. The result is greater goddess connection, reinforcing commitment in a long-term relationship through loving communion, thus enhancing the bond. The second level is spiritual union, which is the ultimate expression of sexuality. Often one receives inspiration and illumination that can be translated into divine guidance or simply experienced as pure bliss. These transcendental sexual experiences produce a sense of merging with the source of energy and losing physical boundaries during orgasm. It is often described as "being in the moment of boundless bliss." Many ancient and modern visionary experiences are described as feelings of being "bathed in pure light." It is cosmic orgasm, the direct experience of the self as pure energy, in union with a divine source.

CHAPTER 7

Ancient Goddesses and Goddess Worship

The Hindu deities are just as much a part of humanity's psychic structure. Like any other powerful symbolic form, the Hindu deities represent and can also uncover helpful psychological forces. They personify the energies that we feel. Then there is the practice of deity meditation, which advanced practitioners in the Tantric traditions have developed into a living science for transforming consciousness.

Deity meditation can help with issues with power or love and call forth specific transformative forces within the mind and heart. It puts us in touch with the protective power within us and can change the way we see the world. This is particularly true of the goddess energies of the Hindu tradition. Durga/Kali, Lakshmi, and Saraswati, according to ancient Hindu teachings, are the personified powers of strength, beauty, and wisdom. The following are the many legends about these goddesses:

Saraswati

Saraswati "the flowing one," dresses in white and holds a book, a rosary, and a stringed instrument called a veena to represent the practice of mantra repletion. Her companion, the swan, is celebrated in Hindu iconography as the bird whose beak can separate the milk of wisdom from the water of material existence, for Saraswati's great gift is the discernment that lets us find divinity in the world. Saraswati is also the deity of language and music, the power behind creative inspiration.

Lakshmi

Lakshmi is "good fortune and the essence of everything we hold desirable. As the deity of wealth, good fortune, and happiness, she stands atop an open lotus flower, as lovely as a Bollywood film star. Gold coins drip from one of her four arms, symbolizing her overflowing generosity. But Lakshmi also gives spiritual gifts — the feeling of bliss, for example, is a sure sign of her subtle presence. One of her other names, Shri means auspiciousness, and everything about this goddess conveys beauty, goodness, and harmony.

However, Lakshmi reminds us that true wealth is not in sheer materialism. Material wealth means nothing if you're not secure on the ground you stand upon. She encourages us to learn the art of not just earning money, but also managing, investing and budgeting it, and most importantly, spending it. Money is just energy. Wealth, however, is the wisdom of harnessing that energy, and the power of being secure on your own two feet—never being dependent on anyone else. Lakshmi also wants us to take care of their bodies and treat it like a temple. After all, beauty is power, especially when it comes from a healthy place.

Durga

Durga means "the unfathomable one" and is the cosmic warrior, the force within consciousness that battles ignorance and darkness. Durga rides a lion, and her arms bristle with weapons, which she uses to slay an assortment of demons and negative forces. Her face, however, shines with peace and compassion.

Durga is the power behind dramatic breakthroughs. She's the strength you can draw on when facing a challenging situation.

Other Goddesses

Eris

Eris is known as the goddess of strife and discord. However, once we remove the patriarchal lens from which she is often viewed, we realize she truly is a goddess of chaos. Chaos is a powerfully magical force that follows no rules— that of man, or God, or time itself. Eris is the goddess who knows how to stir things up. And let's face it, life is chaos. Men strive to bring order to the world by building laws and tenets for people to abide by, policing our individuality, as well as, making life difficult for those who don't abide by it. Eris comes in to remind them that no matter what they do, there will always be a powerful "chaotic" Divine Feminine force that will make patriarchy's mightiest structures crumble and fall, and all that remains shall be dust.

Eris is here to bless women with the ability to embrace their inner chaotic energy and not be limited in any which way. Her greatest gift is the ability to adapt and move on to any and every situation, with minimal damage along the way. The ability to seek thrills (cheap and not so cheap ones) and chase every whim and fancy, with the ability to not get so deep that they sink. Eris will always help Gemini not just survive but also have fun whilst flirting with danger. Honor Eris by honoring your individuality. You and your Queen must explore all horizons and follow all pursuits without worrying about what others may think. Own your "chaotic" multi-talented abilities.

Athena

Athena is the Greek goddess of war and a divine strategist. She is, after all, the goddess of wisdom. Athena was worshipped by armies before heading into wars. Whoever offered the greatest prayers and sacrifices to her was blessed to go on to win. Athena reminds women to honor the strength of their Divine Feminine selves. The best way to honor your connection with Goddess Athena is to forever put your passions, mission, and worth above all else. Honor your individuality and never ever diminish yourself.

Luna

Luna is the Roman goddess of the moon who rides a two-horsed silver chariot called Biga across the night skies. With a crescent moon as her crown, she's often called the "two-horned Queen of the stars," and her dominion covers not only all that happens under the night sky but also all that happens in the depths of the human mind. This is why when we lose control of our minds and our emotional well-being, we enter into a state of "lunacy."

Controlling the tides of the ocean, the cycles of the body, and the potency of the Earth itself, Luna is often considered a powerful figure who commands over the realms of birth and death as well. This is why her changing face was often used by sages to depict not just world events, but also the ideal time to plant seeds, harvest crops, and in some cases, even when to invade countries or even get a haircut when you wish to grow your hair longer, trim it when Luna is new. When you wish for it to grow thicker but slower, trim it when Luna is full. Touch a blade when she's waning, and your hair shall fall fast and shall be frail.

Luna blesses women with a powerful connection to the moon. If they follow the lunar cycles, not only will they be able to master their emotional states, but they'll also find it easier to flow through life. Honor Luna by meditating during full as well as new moons. The former will enable you to become stronger in body and mind. The latter will help battle demons (outer and inner) and enable you to reveal divine sources of creativity and magic itself.

Inanna

The goddess knows that a woman's power comes from owning and taking responsibility for her sexuality and overall life itself. Inanna is the Mesopotamian goddess associated with love, beauty, war, justice, political power, and yes, fertility. Known as, "The Queen of Heaven," Inanna was one of the only deities who could descend into the underworld and return unharmed without a scratch in spite of undergoing hellish levels of torture—including having her corpse hung from a hook. Her love and devotion know no bounds, but at the same time, she remains a Queen in her own right.

Inanna is here to bless women to own their womanhood with pride. Inanna blesses Virgo with the ability to remain unscathed through the best and worst times in life. All they have to do is never compromise our independence and identity—especially for the sake of a man. Be generous and compassionate for sure—but make sure that your own needs are being fulfilled while your voice is being heard. Inanna blesses your Queen with incredible talents in many areas of life—some of which have nothing to do with the other. It is her way of reminding women of their ability to not just successfully adapt to any and every situation but to remain forever self-sufficient.

Aphrodite

Aphrodite is most known for her beauty. Born from the foams of the sea that were mixed with the severed parts of Heaven itself, she emerged out of a shell on the shores of Cyprus. The Greeks worship her as the ultimate Goddess of Love, lust, beauty, passion, pleasure, fertility, and surprisingly—war itself. She was, after all, the reason the Trojan War began.

Jealous and vain to an unapologetic degree, Aphrodite has a surprising streak of fairness which one can only appreciate when looked at from a larger perspective. After all, all is fair in love and in war. This is why she is often connected with divine Justice herself. For some it may seem strange how a fickle goddess represents fairness and justice. Aphrodite, however, considers it part of the beauty and multidimensional powers that come with being a woman.

Aphrodite blesses women to own their femininity and harness their powers freely. Whether it's in the boardroom, bedroom, or battlefield, Queens have Aphrodite's blessings to charm and bewitch even the staunchest rival. Aphrodite gives Libra the ability to see situations from various points of view, giving them the ability to empathize yet strategize wisely. Honor Aphrodite by honoring your beauty — inner and outer. Beauty is strength, beauty is power, and beauty is magic that can be used to empower.

Diana

Diana is the goddess of the hunt, wilderness, animals, moon, and adventure. The Ancient Romans valued her open heart and free spirit. Diana preferred the forests and jungles and found solace with animals of all sorts. Diana was also the most powerful archer, with the power to shoot her arrows with a divine precision that would make mortal heroes and gods quiver with amazement. Diana also rules magic — magic that comes from understanding our divine connection with nature and the various phases of the moon.

Diana is bound to no one and is free to be herself unapologetically. It's no wonder that Wonder Woman herself is named after Diana.

Diana blesses women with the power of aiming high and achieving their dreams. She gives us the freedom to "hunt" for what we want and takes it without any hesitation. She feeds our soul with the thirst for adventure. Diana is honored best when we speak the truth and uplift our fellow beings — especially in the face of opposition.

CHAPTER 8

The Female Orgasm

You will only help your Queen unleash her inner sex goddess through worship, and it is essential you understand everything there is to know about the female orgasm. In a Female Led Relationship, rule number one is sex is for the Queen's pleasure. This means that part of keeping your Queen completely satisfied, happy, and in a great mood every single day is satisfying her by knowing how to give her a great orgasm. Boring sex creates boring relationships, which don't last long. One of the reasons sex tends to get boring very fast is because women are unsatisfied and sexual activities become mundane.

Culture and societal norms teach young women that they will experience sexual pleasure once they have intercourse with a man, but for a very large percentage of women, this is never the case. Women are taught to place their focus on male sexual satisfaction and ignore their own sexual desires. Instead of ensuring that men are taught to focus on a woman's needs so that they both experience pleasure, most women are left unsatisfied because men know very little about the female genitals or female orgasms. Think of how life would be if you could be certain you gave your Queen a mind-blowing orgasm every day. Well, now you can.

Studies show that 74 percent of women have faked an orgasm, so chances are your Queen has as well. Not only is a thorough understanding of the female orgasm going to change the relationship, but you are going to reap the rewards of a happy wife, happy life. Sexual fulfillment is a huge component of overall happiness and well-being, and more women are very interested in how to have better orgasms. As men assuming a more supportive, submissive role in FLR, it is essential you learn everything you can about the female orgasm and how to sexually satisfy your Queen.

Wouldn't you love to have a woman who wakes up singing your praises, who's in a great mood, happy, cheerful, and fully satisfied? This is what the female orgasm will do for your Queen, and it is up to you to provide her with as many as she desires. Despite major advancements in gender equality and women's marches, there is less done for helping women to have more and better female orgasms. In many sex lives, men's happiness still comes first, but FLR and my *Love and Obey* movement aim to change all of this.

I can recall sitting in a sex education lecture learning about the female reproductive system and only being taught from a diagram that showed a long tube in the center with two flaps at the top, which were the female uterus and fallopian tubes. There were never any diagrams of the actual vagina, the clitoris, or the G-spot. These are extremely important parts of the female sex organs, integral to the female orgasm, but were always omitted. Now why is that? We knew everything there was to know about the male penis, erections, and their orgasms, yet virtually nothing about the female orgasm. It's only very recently that we have seen scenes of oral sex for women shown in movies and TV shows when blow jobs for men have been shown for decades.

To me, this was an injustice to women and being able to experience the pleasure they deserve. Times have changed and men have no choice but to learn everything there is to know about cunnilingus and oral sex for women because the smart Queens are demanding sexual satisfaction, and if you're a man and you want to serve and satisfy a great woman, you will dedicate your time to learning all the skills, tip, and tricks necessary to give your Queen the greatest female orgasm.

What is Female Orgasm?

The female orgasm can be seen as a gateway that unlocks a woman's inner goddess. During an orgasm, the body releases hormones such as oxytocin, endorphins, and dopamine that are associated with feelings of pleasure, connection, and euphoria. By allowing herself to experience the physical, mental, and emotional release that comes with an orgasm, a woman can tap into a heightened sense of self-awareness and connection with her surroundings. This can help her open up to new depths of her femininity and power and unlock her inner goddess.

Orgasms have been linked to many positive psychological benefits, such as improved mood, greater life satisfaction, better self-esteem, and increased relationship satisfaction. The female orgasm is when a woman experiences a peak sensation of intense pleasure, creating an altered state of consciousness, usually with an initiation accompanied by involuntary, rhythmic contractions of the vaginal muscles.

Female hysteria was widely recognized as a medical diagnosis from the late 1700s to the early 1900s. It was commonly seen as a form of mental illness that could manifest in physical symptoms. In the late 19th century, it became increasingly associated with the then-emerging field of psychiatry, and eventually its understanding and treatment gradually faded away in the early 1900s.

Female hysteria was a historical diagnosis of women that is no longer recognized in modern medicine. It was thought to involve physical symptoms such as anxiety, nervousness, sleeplessness, irritability, and "sexual desire." The traditional treatment for this condition was pelvic massage to provoke orgasm. Today, treatments for irritability or poor mood often involve therapy and medication, rather than a physical procedure.

Typically, your Queen will be in a relaxed and content mood after enjoying multiple orgasms during a night of lovemaking. She may express herself by showing gratitude and feeling nurtured, as well as feeling an increased sense of connection and intimacy with her partner. She may also feel energized and elated and display a greater sense of confidence and self-worth. She may even be humming or singing her favorite songs in the morning while getting coffee or having breakfast.

Orgasms can empower your Queen. They can bring a greater sense of confidence and euphoria, leading to increased self-esteem and a positive body image. Orgasms can also promote greater self-awareness, providing women with a powerful tool to connect with their own feelings and body. In addition, orgasms can often lead to improved intimacy and connection in relationships, fostering a feeling of trust, love, and understanding. So, it is understandable that on a woman's journey to becoming a Goddess of Love, an exploration of the female orgasm is crucial.

Phases of Arousal

There are four phases of arousal leading to orgasm. The four phases of the female orgasm are:

1. Arousal and Excitement

During the arousal and excitement phase, the body increases its production of hormones like estrogen, oxytocin, dopamine, and endorphins. This results in increased sexual tension and a heightened level of sensitivity in the body, as well as an increase in heart rate, blood flow to the pelvic area, and muscle tension in the clitoral region.

2. Plateau

During this phase, sexual tension builds even more. Your woman will not be able to think of anything other than sexual pleasure. During the plateau phase, the body's responses continue to intensify, and the heart rate, breathing, and muscle tension increase. This is usually the point at which the woman begins to feel the sensations of orgasm.

3. *Orgasm*

The orgasm phase is the climax of sexual pleasure and is characterized by rapid contractions of the muscles in the pelvic area and intense sensations of pleasure. This is often when women experience reflexive movement of the hips, a heightened pulse rate, and involuntary vocalizations. When she reaches orgasm, her vagina, uterus, pelvic floor muscles, and muscles all over your body contract rhythmically.

4. *Resolution*

Finally, the resolution phase is characterized by a gradual reduction in muscle tension and physiological responses, as well as a decrease in arousal. This often results in feelings of relaxation and satisfaction. Following her orgasm, her body relaxes, her heart rate, blood pressure, and breathing slow down to a more normal rate. Pressed or caressed the right way, a woman can be transported to such ecstasy, that for a few seconds, the rest of the world ceases to exist. This feeling is due to the intense pleasure, heightened arousal, and release of endorphins that are experienced during orgasm.

The feeling of the world ceasing to exist is often a result of being completely absorbed in the moment and letting go of all other thoughts and worries. Also, as the tension builds during orgasm, it can be incredibly difficult to think of anything other than the sensations being experienced. But if a man performs incompetently, his woman will be full of frustration and even anger can ensue. Why are orgasms so intensely pleasurable? The orgasm is one of the biggest predictors of sexual satisfaction and ultimately a woman's satisfaction with her relationship as a whole.

The patriarchy has tried to teach us that male sexual desire is stronger and more frequent than females. This is a myth. Studies have actually found that men and women have comparable levels of sexual desire and frequency. Gender differences in sexuality can be attributed to social and cultural influences rather than biology. Studies have also found that women are just as capable or even more so than men of reaching high levels of arousal and sexual pleasure.

Society often expects men to be more sexually driven and aggressive because of the traditional gender roles prescribed to them, while women are typically expected to be more restrained and to fit into a more submissive role. This can be seen in the media, advertising and other cultural messages that perpetuate gender stereotypes. Additionally, cultural norms and expectations also play a huge role in dictating these expectations; when men stray from traditional gendered roles, they often face more criticism and pressure than women who do the same.

Responsive sexual desire is when a person's interest in sexual activity increases when they are presented with a sexual stimulus. There has been a lot of research conducted on how men and women differ in their responsiveness. Generally, men tend to exhibit higher levels of responsive sexual desire than women, often expressed through greater levels of arousal and motivation. On the other hand, women tend to be slower to become aroused and may take longer to experience a sense of readiness for sexual activity. Additionally, women often need to be in the right emotional and physical state in order to experience sexual desire, while men may not necessarily require those same conditions.

Contextual sexual desire is a type of sexual desire that is influenced by factors such as environment, relationship type, physical touch, and clothing. It is associated with the arousal and motivation to engage in sexual activity in response to contextual cues within the environment or the person's relationship. This type of sexual desire is thought to be more present in women, who tend to need and prioritize safety, communication, and trust when engaging in sexual activity. Men, on the other hand, are more likely to prioritize physical arousal and experiences with visual stimuli when considering sexual desire.

Men and women may experience sex differently due to a variety of factors, including social expectations, gender roles, biological differences, and how they were raised. Men may be more likely to focus on physical and visual elements of sex, while women may be more likely to prioritize safety, trust, communication, and emotional connection. Additionally, men tend to experience greater levels of testosterone and other hormones associated with arousal, which may contribute to their different preferences and motivations in sexual encounters.

Barry Komisaruk of Rutgers University in New Jersey found that Queens experience an increase in brain activity across many different regions when aroused, indicating that women may be more capable of processing an array of different sensations and emotions during sex. In contrast, men tend to show more of a localized response to arousal, possibly indicating a more focused experience. These differences in brain activity may explain why men and women experience sex so differently and why women may be more likely to prioritize emotional connection and communication.

Research has demonstrated that women can experience multiple orgasms, which can be attributed to differences in the way their brains process arousal. Many women also report needing continued physical and emotional stimulation in order to reach multiple climaxes. This becomes difficult if the man is focused on himself and achieves a quick orgasm. Men often reach orgasm too quickly and typically need a rest period after orgasm often to the exclusion of the female's orgasm.

Men should learn to focus on the female's climax first so that she can experience multiple orgasms. This will help the woman to be more aroused and relaxed, allowing her to reach deeper levels of pleasure. When a man focuses on the female's pleasure first, she usually experiences an orgasm and increases her chances of having multiple orgasms. Additionally, it helps to promote mutual feelings of satisfaction and pleasure for both partners. If a man climaxes too quickly, as is often the case, they will need a rest period after orgasm. This is because the body needs time to recover after the physical and mental energy expended during orgasm.

During this rest period, the body releases hormones that help the person to feel satisfied and relaxed. However, the Queen is left feeling unsatisfied and wondering why the experience was so brief. It is important for men to take the time to focus on their female's pleasure first, and once an orgasm is reached for them to still pay attention to their female's desire for more orgasms. This allows both partners to enjoy the experience to its fullest, instead of having the female feeling left out and unsatisfied.

CHAPTER 9

Types of Female Orgasms

F emale orgasms are the gateway to your goddess's connection to the divine and universal energy. The submissive, supportive gentleman is responsible for unleashing her sex goddess and ensuring she is sexually satisfied. To do this. you must learn everything possible about all types and ways to achieve a female orgasm.

The Clitoris

The clitoris is the primary organ responsible for female orgasm. The clitoris is a highly sensitive organ located at the top of the vulva. Stimulating the clitoris directly or indirectly can cause a woman to experience intense pleasure and orgasm. The clitoris is composed of erectile tissue that grows in size when aroused, allowing it to become highly sensitive and easily stimulated. When properly stimulated, the clitoris can provide a powerful orgasmic response.

Some of the most commonly used nicknames for the clitoris include "love button," "pleasure button," "magic button," and "little bud." It swells when aroused and can provide intense pleasure and orgasm when stimulated properly. While the clitoris may look a bit different from person to person, the basic anatomy is the same for all women. Some women may have larger or more prominent clitorises than others. However, the size or appearance of the clitoris is usually not indicative of a person's level of sexual pleasure or orgasm potential.

The clitoris contains a bundle of nerve endings and is located in the front of her and under the clitoral hood — the triangle part of female genitals that connects to the labia. The clitoris, like the penis, will swell, enlarge, and become more sensitive as your woman becomes more sexually aroused. The most common types of clitoral stimulation that lead to female orgasm are manual stimulation (using one's fingers or a sex toy) and oral stimulation (using the tongue or lips). Other forms of stimulation, such as tapping, rubbing, and vibrating can also be used to bring a woman to orgasm. Many women find that combining multiple types of stimulation in different patterns can be particularly pleasurable and lead to a more intense orgasm.

Stimulation of the clitoris is probably the easiest way for most people to experience an orgasm. It is important to note that the clit is where the excitement begins and often ends. Seven out of ten women said that they required clitoral stimulation to orgasm during sex worship or at the very least clitoral stimulation improves their orgasms.

Never forget clitoral stimulation during sex worship. First thing's first: the vast majority of women require external clitoral stimulation to reach orgasm. In fact, a study of more than 1,000 women in 2017 revealed that only 18 percent of participants could orgasm through vaginal intercourse alone.

So, when you're having sex worship, you want to focus on external clitoral stimulation either alone or in combination with some form of penetration.

When you stimulate the clitoris with your finger, it is important to use a slow, gentle, circular motion that gradually increases in intensity. Use enough pressure to stimulate the clitoris, but be careful not to be too rough or extreme. Start by using a single finger and then gradually increase the pressure, adding additional fingers and varying the pattern. Keep the clitoris lubricated by using a water-based lubricant to ensure maximum comfort. As your Queen becomes aroused, you should increase the frequency and intensity of the stimulation until she reaches orgasm.

When using a vibrator, start off on a low setting and then gradually increase the speed or intensity as she becomes aroused. She should experiment with different areas of her clitoris and find the spot that gives her the most pleasure. As she nears orgasm, she can experiment with different vibration combos and speeds until she finds what works best. Your Queen should focus on her breath and let the vibrations take her over the edge. She can also place the vibrator on her body in different places to explore different sensations. When she is ready for an orgasm, she can either stay in the same setting or increase the vibration until her orgasm is reached.

A woman can achieve orgasm with the use of the palm of your hand. You should start by lightly caressing her clitoris in circular motions, gradually increasing pressure and speed as she builds arousal. Once she is aroused, you can press your palm against her clitoris and move it in circles or up and down in a rhythmical motion. You can also experiment with using different parts of your palm, such as your thumb and the index finger to create stronger and more direct stimulation. As she nears orgasm, she can focus on her breath, and you can increase the pressure and speed of your hand until orgasm is reached.

She can also achieve orgasm with your tongue by carefully stimulating the clitoris with gentle licks and flicks of the tip. You should start by lightly running the tip of your tongue over the clitoris and labia in circles and then increasing the pressure and speed as she builds arousal. Once she is aroused, you can use the flat of your tongue to cover the clitoris and gently apply pressure using a slow, circular motion. You can also experiment with different tongue shapes, like zig zags or figure-eight patterns to create stronger and more direct stimulation. As she nears orgasm, she can focus on her breathing and you can increase the pressure and speed of your tongue until orgasm is reached.

Using the mouth to achieve orgasm is a pleasurable and powerful experience. Wrap your lips around the shaft of the clitoris and gently suck, creating a vacuum. Then, you can use your tongue to swirl around the tip of the clitoris, flicking, and sucking up and down. You can also use her hands to press against the labia, providing additional stimulation and pressure. As your Queen becomes more aroused, you can increase the speed and pressure of the sucking and licking. When she approaches orgasm, she can focus on her breath and increase the suction of your mouth to increase the pleasure until she climaxes. To get more in-depth information about oral sex worship, read my book *Oral Sex for Women*. It discusses various techniques and positions that your goddess will find enjoyable.

Vaginal Orgasm

A vaginal orgasm is an orgasm that occurs through stimulation of only the vagina usually through penetration. It is caused by stimulation of the vaginal walls and the internal areas near the cervix. It may involve a feeling of release and pleasure in the pelvic area. It may also involve sensations of warmth, fullness, and an all-over sensual pleasure. A vaginal orgasm is an intense and pleasurable sensation and can be enhanced when the clitoris is stimulated along with the inner vagina during penetrative sex.

The clitoris can be indirectly involved in a vaginal orgasm when the walls of the vagina are stimulated during sexual activity. This stimulation may cause the internal areas surrounding the clitoris to become more sensitive and responsive to stimulation. This can lead to increases in blood flow and increased nerve endings, many of which may cause the clitoris to become more aroused and create a stronger orgasm.

Some of the best sexual positions to combine both vaginal and clitoral stimulation include cowgirl, missionary, doggy style, and reverse cowgirl. Cowgirl position can be modified to provide both vaginal and clitoral stimulation by having the receiver lean forward for more pressure on the clitoris. The missionary position can be adjusted to provide stimulation on the clitoris through direct gentle rubbing of that area. Doggy style can provide both vaginal and clitoral stimulation through more intense thrusting and grinding. Reverse cowgirl also allows for increased clitoral stimulation as the receiver can lean back and forth to add pressure to that area.

During penetrative sex, you can also give your goddess wonderful orgasms by stimulating the G-spot. It is an area located on the anterior wall of the vagina, about two to three inches up. It is a spongy patch of tissue that is full of nerve endings and when stimulated can cause powerful and pleasurable sensations for the person receiving stimulation. The G-spot is most likely to be found if pressure is applied in a "come-hither" motion using the fingers or a curved toy. One of the best sexual positions for stimulating the G-spot during penetrative vaginal sex is doggy style. Doggy style allows for deeper penetration than other positions, making it more likely to hit the G-spot. Other positions that can be used to stimulate the G-spot in this way include spooning, cowgirl, reverse cowgirl, and the position where the woman sits on the partner's lap.

There is also one more technique that is guaranteed to drive your sex goddess wild. The A-spot is an erogenous zone at the end of the vagina near the cervix. The A-spot is a relatively newly discovered erogenous zone, and so relatively little is known about it. It is not widely discussed in popular culture, and it has only recently been studied in scientific studies. It can be reached by curved toys and fingers, and gently stroking the area can create powerful and pleasurable sensations. The best toys feature unique curves and angles to reach deep within the vagina and access the A-spot. A-spot stimulation can be particularly effective during extended foreplay and can intensify orgasm when stimulated.

Cervical Orgasm

Cervical stimulation has the potential to lead to a full-body orgasm that can send waves of tingly pleasure up and down the body for your woman. And this is an orgasm that can keep on giving, lasting quite a while for some. A cervical orgasm creates a full-body orgasm by sending waves of pleasure through the entire body. This type of orgasm begins in the pelvic area, but can be felt throughout, as the uterus contracts, stimulating nerve endings all over the body. The intense pleasure that is felt can cause contractions throughout the entire body, creating an incredibly intense and satisfying full body orgasm.

Cervical orgasms are powerful orgasms that happen as a result of stimulation of the cervical area, located at the top of the vaginal canal near the uterus. It is a highly sensitive area, and stimulation of it can bring about a much more intense orgasm experience that can last for 20 seconds or more. These types of orgasms are credited with giving your Queen the "Big One" because of the intensity of the pleasure and the wide array of sensations that can occur.

Some sex positions that are well known in achieving a cervical orgasm include:

- **Spooning.** This position allows for slow and gentle thrusting, which can be effective in stimulating the cervix.

- **Cowgirl.** This position gives the woman control over the speed and depth of penetration, making it easier to reach her cervix.

- **Reverse Cowgirl.** Similar to Cowgirl, this position gives the woman control and allows for different angles of penetration.

- **Doggy Style**. This position allows for deeper penetration and allows the man to control the pace, depth, and angle of thrusting.

- **Butterfly**. This position also provides different angles and depths of penetration, allowing for maximum cervical stimulation.

CHAPTER 10

History of the Female Orgasm

I t wasn't until the 16th century that the clitoris began to be described as a distinct physical structure, common to all women, with the function of inducing pleasure. In 1559, Realdo Colombo described the clitoris as "the seat of a woman's delight." Yet in subsequent centuries, female pleasure took a back seat, and the clitoris was forgotten. It re-emerged in the 20th century. Though Sigmund Freud at least acknowledged that women could experience orgasm, he believed that clitoral responsivity is superseded by vaginal orgasm in mature women. Freud believed that the inability to experience vaginal orgasms is associated with psychosexual immaturity.

From the 19th to the mid-20th centuries, many psychologists, inspired by Freudian psychoanalysis, argued that women should only achieve orgasm through vaginal penetration by a man. Any other kind of female sexual pleasure—including masturbation, queer sexuality, and any stimulation of the clitoris—was considered a sign of "masculinity," imbalance, or even insanity.

In the last chapter we discussed hysteria, a so-called mental illness which supposedly resulted from excess female sexual desire. The "treatment" for hysteria was orgasm stimulated by a doctor or even the horrifying removal of the clitoris entirely. It was in this atmosphere of stigma that the father of modern psychology, Sigmund Freud, produced his influential work. According to Freud, while female children experienced pleasure from the clitoris, adult women had to shift their focus exclusively to vaginal intercourse or risk psychological disorder.

As a result, until the mid-twentieth century, psychologists considered women who orgasmed from clitoral stimulation immature and even prone to psychosis. "Proper" sexual pleasure was defined only through married, vaginal heterosexual intercourse. Women who couldn't orgasm this way were often considered frigid, disordered, or automatically assumed to be lesbian, which was also considered a mental illness.

Feminists Support

With the sexual revolution of the sixties, feminists and researchers embarked on a mission to reclaim the clitoris. In psychology, the pioneering sexuality research of William Masters and Virginia Johnson challenged the theoretical ideas of Freud by using direct observation to study a wide range of human sexual experiences. Their more woman-centered approach saw women's sexuality as important in and of itself, not as a mere reflection of their male partners.

Second wave feminists virulently critiqued the idea that female sexuality should be centered around married,

heterosexual vaginal intercourse. Feminists like Luce
Irigaray, Monique Wittig, and Adrienne Rich argued that the
Freudian focus on the vagina was simply a way to make
women subservient to men. They argued variously for a
reclaiming of the clitoris as the source of women's pleasure
and orgasm, for a more holistic experience of sensuality
beyond the genitals, and for the liberating potential of
lesbianism.

Other feminists didn't merely write about female sexual
pleasure—they showed women how to obtain it. The Boston
Women's Health Collective pioneered medically accurate,
frank, and sex-positive information about sexuality with their
1971 publication of *Our Bodies, Ourselves*, which is still in
print. Tee Corinne's 1975 *Cunt Coloring Book* celebrated the
diversity of vulvas (not just vaginas) with detailed
illustrations. And starting from the late sixties, sex educator
Betty Dodson began championing the transformative power
of women's masturbation through writing and group
masturbation workshops—with much emphasis on the
wonders of the clitoris.

History of the G-spot

For a long time, the "G-spot" was the prime target. The
term was first coined in the early 80s, for the German
obstetrician and gynecologist, Ernst Gräfenberg. In 1950, he
described an erogenous zone on the anterior, or front wall of
the vagina, which correlated with the position of the urethra
on the other side of that wall. Subsequent studies revealed a
complex of blood vessels, nerve endings and remnants of the
female prostate gland in the same area; and suggested that in
a minority of women—particularly those with strong pelvic

floor muscles — stimulation of this area could trigger powerful orgasms and the release of a small amount of fluid from the urethra that was not urine.

Word soon began to leak out about this magic button on the front wall of the vagina. Couples invested time and effort into finding it. Meanwhile, some feminists claimed that the publicity surrounding the G-spot was an attempt by men to recoup the importance of vaginal penetration, after the spotlight had shifted to the clitoris during the sexual revolution of the 60s and 70s.

One of the first researchers to prove vaginal orgasms existed is Barry Komisaruk, who took the first steps to answering these questions by chance, while he was studying mating behaviors in rats. One day, while inserting a rod into a female rat's vagina, he triggered a bizarre response. The rats became rigidly immobile. During this kind of stimulation, the rats became apparently insensitive to pain. Soon afterwards, he switched his rats for women, and noticed the same thing: vaginal stimulation blocked the transmission of pain.

Komisaruk conducted a study with Beverly Whipple that looked at women with varying degrees of spinal cord injury. They found that even when their injuries blocked the known nerve pathways in the spinal cord from the genitals to the brain, these women could still feel when their vagina and cervix were being touched. Some even experienced orgasm from it, despite the pudendal nerve — which carries sensations from the clitoris to the brain — being cut. Women with spinal cord injury who could not feel their clitoris, nevertheless had orgasms from vaginal stimulation. The reason is that the vagus nerves, which are situated outside the spinal cord, carry sensations from the vagina to the brain.

Women describe clitoral orgasms as more localized and external, and vaginal orgasms as being internal and involving the whole-body; that's probably because the nerves that carry sensations from the clitoris are different from the nerves from the vagina. And as for the fact that vaginal orgasms can block pain, the nerves connected to the spinal cord may inhibit the release of the neurotransmitter involved in pain perception. Once signals reach the brain, they could also trigger the release of neurotransmitters like endorphins that also relieve pain.

Taoist Sexual Spiritual Practice

Taoists may practice sexual spirituality and goddess worship. These practices are known as "joining energy" or "the joining of the essences." Practitioners believe that by performing these sexual arts, one can stay in good health, and attain longevity and spiritual advancement. Taoists view sexual intercourse as an opportunity to connect and open up spiritually. This practice is thought to be a way to honor yourself and your goddess, and release divine energy during sex. It is said that when practiced consciously, two individuals can become deeply connected and can use divine energy created by sexual arousal and orgasm to create a sacred union. Taoists emphasize setting a gentle and loving tone for sexual practices and maintaining a respectful attitude throughout.

Héqì is a spiritual practice developed during the Han Dynasty. It was originally a Chinese Taoist tradition that combines the principles of external massage and internal breathing techniques, with the goal of using the sexual energy created by intercourse to reach a deeper connection and heightened spiritual state. The technique involves carefully controlled breathing and mental focus, alongside physical stimulation that is designed to induce a spiritual and meditative state. This practice is believed to create a deeper connection between two individuals and an increased awareness of the divine within each individual. It is said that the practice is both calming and invigorating, and can produce a heightened sense of intimacy, love, and spiritual connection.

Qi is an ancient Chinese philosophical concept describing a type of energy that is thought to permeate the universe. The concept of Qi is central to traditional Chinese medicine and an integral part of traditional Chinese culture, where it is seen as an integral component of a person's health and well-being. In Chinese spiritual traditions, it is believed that by cultivating and circulating this energy, an individual can achieve increased spiritual awareness, balance, and health.

During sexual worship, a man should control his orgasm, and even avoid it. The Taoist practice of withholding jing or semen is known as the "jade pillow practice," and is believed to be beneficial to men in multiple ways. It is believed to improve physical stamina and mental alertness, increase life force energy, promote relaxation, and stimulate healing. Additionally, it is thought to help men to better circulate their energy, improve focus and concentration, and even enhance creativity. Finally, some believe that controlling semen allows a man to conserve vital energy resources and store that energy in his body rather than allowing it to be lost through ejaculation.

The "jade pillow practice" is commonly used as part of sexual goddess worship, as it is seen as a way to honor the divine energy of the goddess and to honor one's own spiritual connections in the process. By refraining from ejaculating during sexual activities, a man is seen to be honoring the goddess and the sacred energy of the act. It is also believed that by withholding the ejaculate, a man is able to better channel his energy into his goddess and develop an even deeper spiritual connection with her. Additionally, it is thought that when a man can control and preserve his jing, or semen, he is better able to honor the Divine Feminine energy present in sexual goddess worship.

Taoists practice of sexual goddess worship include:

- **Making offerings.** This is often done during ritual or ceremony as a way of expressing gratitude and appreciation for the goddess.

- **Mindful meditation.** By engaging in mindful meditation, it is believed to help open one's heart to the spiritual energies of the goddess.

- **Visualization.** Through the practice of visualization, practitioners can imagine themselves in a sacred and serene space of the goddess, creating a connection between the individual and the spiritual realm.

- **Chanting mantras.** This is viewed as a way to open oneself to the energy of the goddess.

  i. Om Aim Saraswati Maha-Shaktiye Namaha – This is a mantra dedicated to Saraswati, the Hindu goddess of knowledge and wisdom.

ii.   Om Kali Ma – This mantra honors the Hindu goddess Kali, the destroyer of ignorance and illusion.

iii.   Om Aing Sreem Hreem Shreem Kleem – This mantra is dedicated to the Hindu Goddess Lakshmi, the goddess of abundance and prosperity.

- **Writing poetry.** The writing of poetry can be used as a way of expressing feelings and emotions dedicated to the goddess.

- **Tantric practices.** Tantric practices are believed to facilitate the connection between the physical and spiritual world through the act of sexual union.

For Taoists, sex worship is not just about pleasing a gentleman but is focused on female pleasure. Rituals include appreciation of a woman's body, kissing, gently stimulating her clit, and/or stimulating her G-spot. The purpose is to experience pleasure and cultivate energy and power through sexual encounters. Huangdi, the Yellow Emperor, noted ten important indications of female satisfaction. If sex worship were performed properly, the goddess will create more Divine Feminine energy, and the supportive gentleman will easily absorb this energy to increase his own power and connection to the goddess.

Here are the Yellow Emperor's ten indications of proper goddess sex worship:

1. Increased frequency and intensity of moaning sounds

2. Suppressing any urge to move the hips

3. Heightened awareness and increased eye contact

4. Tensing of the leg muscles

5. Openness in her pelvic area and hips

6. Lowering of her breathing rate

7. Changes in complexion and increased sweating

8. Loss of the sense of time

9. Softening and relaxation of the body

10. Release of vaginal bodily fluids

A man can use sex worship to extend his own life by engaging in sexual activity that is pleasurable, focusing on his Queen's pleasure, and cultivating mind-body connection. This could include taking time to honor and appreciate his partner, exploring different techniques of lovemaking, and adopting a practice of intentional and purposeful communication throughout the experience. Sex worship can lead to greater intimacy, improved communication, heightened arousal, and release of feel-good hormones, leading to improved physical and psychological well-being, which can help achieve greater longevity.

Ancient texts often describe the power of sex worship as a form of spiritual communion and intimate exchange between a man and a woman. Many religious traditions believed that during sex, a man and woman's energies could merge and mingle, creating an energetic bridge between the genders that could nurture the soul, heal the body, and extend life.

In Taoism, the term "the battle of stealing and strengthening" is used to describe the act of sex worship, as it is seen as an intense battle of energy exchange between the two parties. During the sexual act, both individuals are thought to be vying for control and dominance of their partner's energies. In Taoism, the battle of stealing and strengthening is explained as the process by which one partner can "steal" some of the other's person's energy, and in order to do so, they must be able to "strengthen" their own energy, be able to hold it, and then transfer it to their partner. Taoists believe that the stronger a person's own energy is, the more they can successfully "steal" and "strengthen" their partner's energy. Doing this through the act of sex worship can ultimately lead to greater spiritual, physical, and emotional well-being.

In Taoism, sex worship is believed to benefit the goddess. It is believed that the goddess can receive energy sourced from the male worshipper, which will make her more powerful and increase her ability to bring life, harmony, and growth to a family, community, and the world. Additionally, by becoming the object of worship by her man, the goddess is believed to gain the power to bring healing, peace, and prosperity to their relationship. It is also believed that sex worship can help the goddess gain a deeper understanding of her own power and sexuality, as well as increase her level of creativity and wisdom.

Goddess worship is believed to be an empowering and even sacred activity for the goddess. It is thought to help her reach the highest levels of pleasure and enlightenment, as well as connect her with the source of her power. It is also believed to balance her masculine and feminine energy and bring her closer to the divine. Furthermore, the goddess is believed to gain insight from this sexual practice, as it provides her with a deeper understanding of her spiritual and biological nature, as well as helping her to manifest her gifts and creativity.

There is also great news for men who engage in goddess sex worship. Through the act of sex worship, a man could regain his youth and longevity by embracing the woman's energy as "the divine energy of creation," which could be harvested during intercourse and transferred to him. In Kama Sutra, it suggests that during sexual intercourse, a man could "absorb the divine energy of the goddess residing within the woman," and it could invigorate him and contribute to his long life.

Other ancient texts, such as The Sutras, explain that sex worship should be used to "liberate the energy within oneself and draw on the infinite energy of the Universe," which could help extend a man's life. It shows that goddess worship is a powerful and beneficial practice for both genders that can increase spiritual, physical, and emotional well-being, and ultimately extend a man's life.

CHAPTER 11

Unlock Her Sex Goddess

Only you, the submissive supportive gentleman, can help your Queen unleash her sex goddess and step into her power as Goddess of Love. A goddess is a woman who emerges from deep within herself. She unleashes a freedom and fearlessness to be herself. She is a woman who can align with the magnificent possibilities within her. She is a woman who knows of the magic and mystery inside her. A woman who can walk into a room and exude an aura of confidence, beauty, and power. It takes on a whole new level when that woman wants to share that energy and knowledge to lift up and empower all of the women around her.

A Queen who is a goddess means having a sense of self-empowerment, self-confidence, and inner strength, as well as having a spiritual connection or to a higher power. When your Queen is a goddess, it means you hold her in high regard and view her as special and unique. She is a magnetic woman who radiates light. When she walks into a room, males and females sense her presence. She has power and softness at the same time. She has powerful sexual energy that's not dependent on physical looks. She has a body that she adores, and it shows by the way she comfortably lives and moves in it. She cherishes beauty, light and love. She is a mother to all children. She flows with life in effortless grace.

When you help your Queen unlock her the sex goddess, you also reawaken your lives as a whole. Your lovemaking is seen as your journey together in exploration of the deeper aspects of your intimacy. You will be responsible for helping your Queen free herself and explore the deeper parts of her sexual desire, needs, and fantasies. This is how she will unleash her sex goddess. She must be allowed to fully experience all of her deepest sexual desires and find her own methods of connecting with the divine. Much like a lab assistant helps the scientist use his or her own genius to lead to discoveries, so too must you assist your Queen to find her own true meaning of goddess. You both must find ways to heighten your sexual experience.

In the state of our true orgasmic energy, we have enormous amounts of power to create the lives we desire. It creates a beautiful orgasmic energy that can be used to not only connect you and your Queen but also can help us create the lives of our dreams. This applies to all intimacy and the energy that is created in these intimate moments. It's as simple as sex creating positive feelings, and positive feelings creating our lives. During moments of true bliss, we lose all ego, and we break into the spiritual realm and are wholly open. This openness is where our divine inspiration and manifestation is created. If you've ever had a soul-shaking orgasm, then you know what I mean when I say that it is a rebirthing process.

A sex goddess is fiercely sensual and fearlessly erotic. She engages in sex as her way to share with another in touching the divine. She is compassionate and has wisdom. She is a seeker of truth and cares deeply about something bigger than herself. She is a woman who knows that her purpose in life is to reach higher and rule with love. She is a woman in love with love. She knows that joy is her destiny and by embracing it and sharing it with others, wounds are healed.

She is a woman who can accept herself as she is. She can accept another as they are. She is a woman who can ask for help when she needs it or give help when asked. She respects boundaries, hers and another's. She is a woman who takes responsibility for everything she creates in her life. She is a woman who is totally supportive and giving. She is a goddess.

Some of the qualities you can help your goddess to achieve are the following:

- **Confidence:** A woman who is self-assured and comfortable in her own skin can be seen as dominant.

- **Assertiveness:** A woman who can express her needs and desires in a clear and direct way can be seen as dominant.

- **Leadership skills:** A woman who can take charge and guide others can be seen as dominant.

- **Decisiveness:** A woman who can make decisions quickly and confidently can be seen as dominant.

- **Emotional intelligence:** A woman who can understand and control her own emotions, as well as read and respond to the emotions of others.

Our sexual energy is our life energy, so when we are disconnected from our sex, we are disconnected from our lives and the deepest parts of ourselves. If your Queen is unsatisfied during sex, she feels disconnected from the divine and a great deal of resentment begins to set in. It begins to destroy the bond you have as a couple because you lack this important point of intimacy and deep bonding. When we are unbalanced in our sexual energy, we end up unbalanced in our chakras, and thus, our energy as a whole. When we are disconnected from our sexual energy, it impacts our relationships, making it almost impossible to connect fully with another. It is easier to fall into the traps of our egos, and we aren't able to see the other person or ourselves in their entirety. We end up denying our own shame and conditioning, which keeps us from delving into our deepest levels of spirituality and pleasure.

The difference with using your sexual experience to help your Queen unlock her sex goddess is that sex becomes a time of deep worship and is a conscious act. When consciousness is the focus during sex, it increases the intensity of the experience. Sex becomes mind-blowing and deeply satisfying. You and your goddess feel like you've been transported to paradise each and every time. Picture if you will, the garden of Eden, a beautiful place, pristine, hidden, gorgeous views, surrounded by plants and flowers, and maybe a stream or waterfall, A perfect place.

Picture you and your Queen enjoying and experiencing each other with total abandon. This is what sex should feel like with your sex goddess. Women are rejuvenated through sex, but they are also inspired and motivated when they receive proper sexual worship and sexual fulfillment. This is important because the more we understand the connection between helping your Queen to step into her role as goddess, it leads to a more fulfilling life. You will feel motivated and committed to serving and worshipping your Queen. Life has meaning. It is imperative to take the time to truly check in with your body, mind, and soul to see if all are in alignment with your sexual energy. Once you are engaged in sex, remain aware of her body and its responses and changes in response. By tuning into your own body's responses and hers, you will form a deeper state of connection and find your intimacy moving deeper than you ever thought possible.

In a Female Led Relationship, rule number one is sex is for the Queen's pleasure. Many submissive men are reporting better sex and less premature ejaculation just by slowing down the entire sexual session and focusing solely on worshipping the Queen. When you switch from sex and the mechanics of having sex to learning how to worship her with all of your tips, tricks, and techniques at your disposal, sex becomes a means of connecting with your Queen and bringing her levels of pleasure she has never experienced before. If you're a man who is serious about changing your sex life and you are focused on increasing your Queen's pleasure, then you need these sex techniques.

First, begin with a warm-up. What are you doing exactly? Are you giving her a few kisses, then undressing and getting on top of her as fast as possible? Or are you spending time, setting the scene, massaging her neck, lower back, thighs— her entire body. Are you placing her in a relaxed position, then taking time to explore her erogenous zones? Spending time in warm-up cannot be underestimated. Whether she feels relaxed, aroused, and purring is going to make a huge difference in the overall sexual satisfaction she gains from your worship. Are you kissing her all over her body to awaken those erogenous zones, managing her breasts, keeping her body warm and tingly?

As you make your way down to her pleasure center, are you maintaining eye contact noting her moans and how her body responds to your touch? If you don't know what is happening while you pleasure your Queen, how will you gauge the success of your sex techniques? There should be improvement from last week to this week, and if there isn't, then you need to change your techniques. The new year is a great way to start learning new techniques to simulate and increase your Queen's sexual arousal.

Are you great or mediocre at oral sex? Now this isn't what you think you are but rather how she thinks *you* are. Are you gaining confirmation from your Queen that you have satisfied her with your oral sex techniques? Does your Queen have mind-blowing orgasms from your oral sex? This is important and it is your job to make sure that you are elevating your oral sex techniques and giving your Queen the goddess worship she deserves.

Next is penetration. How are you transitioning from oral to penetration? Are you fast like a jackhammer where you're just getting in her and you're thrusting like a dog in heat? Or are you controlling your thrusting and controlling the speed and the intensity while gauging your Queen's response. Some Queens desire hard, deep picking and others prefer light and sensuous. Some Queens want coupling where you thrust then hold your thrust and penis in her in a deep way for a few minutes. This sends her into orbit. In my book *Oral Sex for Women* and my book *Female Led Relationship*, I discuss all of these techniques in detail, plus everything to do with Queen worship.

Additional Tips

Here are some additional tips on how to help your Queen become a true sex goddess and ensure sexual satisfaction:

- Make your Queen feel deeply desired and sexy. Compliment her, let her know how much you desire to sexually serve her. Tell her what you plan to do for her and keep the whole day sexy.

- Build intense sexual tension. Look her deep in the eyes when she speaks, pay attention, laugh, touch her, even when you are just hanging out together. Smack her butt, touch her hair, hold her hand. Regardless of how long you've been together, taking some time for some PDA or showing signs of affection is crucial.

- Spend time having lots of foreplay. Instead of diving into sex, try spending lots of time engaging in foreplay. Kissing, cuddling, fondling, massaging. I write extensively in my books about setting the scene and using the right toys, role play, and lots of other sexy sexual arousing activities. Women need to be warmed up and the key to making her horny and desperately craving you, is to warm her up and allow her to build that intense desire for you.

- Switch things up. It is important to switch up position locations, toys, and techniques during sex. We all have busy lives but just as we don't enjoy doing the same activities every weekend, we don't want to do the same things over and over during sex. This is a recipe for disaster because humans can be creatures of habit, but habit leads to boredom and monotony, and soon there is a desire to seek outside adventure. Your sexy adventure needs to be with your Queen, so exploring all sorts of ways to spice up sex and sexual arousal will lead to a much more satisfying sex life.

Keep sexy the focus of your relationship or marriage. Learn what really turns her on. If you're not sure what makes your Queen horny, ask your goddess what turns her on. (Some women may simply get turned on being asked what turns them on.) It shows that you care about her pleasure and want her to have the best sexual experience possible, not to mention it maximizes your likelihood of success. Does she enjoy certain positions over others? Does she enjoy having a few glasses of wine before dinner or does she need a bubble bath? Learn what really turns her on and do these things religiously. Anticipate her needs, show her she is appreciated, touch her, and keep your focus on her.

CHAPTER 12

Tantric Sex Orgasms

The next step to help your Queen become the ultimate sex goddess is to explore how to achieve Tantric sex orgasms. The first step in Tantra is to focus on breathing. Breath in Tantric sex is an important tool to shape both your energies. Your Queen must visualize breathing in from her sex chakra and breathing out from her heart chakra, and for you it is the opposite. The idea is to let every bit of the sexual energy flow through you. This helps in enabling a full-body orgasm because every part of your body is making love. In Tantric sex manifestos, the sex or the sacral chakra is located below the navel while the heart chakra is, well, located at the heart. You must visualize your breath flowing in and out of these chakras.

Tantric Sex Orgasm – Power of Breathing

Tantric is an ancient practice with Buddhist and Hindu origins. Tantra means "woven together." The idea is the metaphor of weaving man and woman together through the physical body. It also relates to the concept of weaving together the physical and the spiritual. Tantra uses the breath, as do other yogic practices, to engage mindfulness. It allows for a heightened awareness of both you and your Queen's emotional and spiritual states during the act of lovemaking.

Tantra also embodies the metaphor of weaving the human to the divine. The practice is meant to allow you both to become one with the god-state. The act of love is likened to worshipping your Queen as your temple. The act of Tantric lovemaking inspires a sacred bond, by heightening intimacy to a divine level. Tantra also increases awareness of your bodies and your own spiritual connection to sex. Through worship of the sacred bond of love, you and your Queen should experience extreme orgasms. These orgasms are powerful, and in some cases, can last for hours.

It's important to remember that prolonged orgasm is not the point of the practice. Sex is often thought to just be a physical act involving the genitals, but the reality is that the hottest sex happens when mind and body are synchronized. This is why breathing and focusing on prolonging the pleasure as in Tantric Sex can change everything for your Queen's orgasms. Your breath impacts your interpretation of sensations and helps to put your mind into a state conducive to experiencing pleasure.

You can help your Queen to focus on breathing by doing the following. Place your hand on her belly. Have her breathe in deeply through her nose, such that you can feel your hand rise and fall as she inhales and exhales. Make sure she is completely relaxed. Deep slow breathing intensifies her orgasms and can result in multiple climaxes.

Positions for Tantric Sex Orgasm

One of the best positions for you and your Queen to practice Tantric sex is the yab-yum position where your Queen sits on your lap, like a lotus, wrapping her legs firmly around you. Your chakras are perfectly aligned in this position, and you are physically touching each other's forehead, heart, and genitals. The intimate connection becomes evenly spread across the body.

Preparation

Tantra is a spiritual practice, which means your mind comes into play as much as your body. When you practice Tantra, you connect your body, mind, and soul. A clear mindset and willingness to step out of your comfort zone are important to uniting those parts of yourself.

Some people find that spending 10 to 15 minutes in meditation can help prepare your mind for Tantra practice, as it allows you to go inward and examine your thoughts.

Prepare Your Space

- Make sure your space is at a comfortable temperature. If it's cold, turn on the heat an hour before your practice so that your room is cozy and warm. If it's hot, turn on the air conditioner, but set it to the high 70s, so that the space is cool, but not chilly.

- Set the mood with candles or tinted light bulbs. Candlelight will add romance to the space, while soft red bulbs will give the area a sensual touch.

- Fill the space with your favorite scent. Light a scented candle, diffuse an essential oil, burn incense sticks, or hang flowers. Pick a smell that makes you feel sexy but isn't overwhelming.

- Soften your space. Lay down a satin throw blanket and a few plush cushions.

- Create a romantic or sexual vibe. Playing some music that you can move to, either by yourself or with a partner.

Tantric Massage

Tantric Massage is a massage technique that involves your full body—including your intimate areas. The goal is to awaken your sexual energy, deepen the intimacy between you and your partner, and increase mindfulness of sexual pleasure and your body. Unlike most other massage methods, Tantric massage incorporates spiritual elements like mindfulness, eye contact, and breathing techniques. Tantric massage involves your erogenous zones and genitals, but the goal isn't to have an orgasm. It's possible to have an orgasm during the massage, but the focus is on giving your goddess the ultimate pleasure.

How to Give a Tantric Massage

- Set up a comfortable space with dimmed lights and relaxing music.

- While making steady eye contact, take five synchronized deep breaths together.

- Focus on your breathing and hers. You want to get into a meditative space.

- Take a natural massage oil like coconut oil and rub it in your hands until it's warm.

- With your goddess lying on her stomach, start massaging the upper areas of her body including their neck, ears, and back.

- Have your goddess flip onto their back and massage the whole body, including the chest, stomach, arms, and legs.

- Next start massaging her inner thighs, moving into the pubic area.

- Move through all of your goddess's erogenous zones, which can include breasts, vulva, butt, perineum, testicles, and penis.

- Communicate with her about what feels good.

- If your partner orgasms, keep massaging them for a few minutes while they cool down. If your goddess isn't aroused, help her to slowly calm their sexual energy until they are relaxed.

Once you have completed this full body experience you can move to breast massage, oral worship and more.

CHAPTER 13

Female Led Relationship & Goddess Sex

A significant part of finding and keeping a goddess in a Female Led Relationship is that a man must show his complete service to her. Part of this service is being a great lover and goddess sex. Why has Casanova been remembered for centuries? Not because he was great at his job or he could fix cars. If you're going to keep your goddess happy, you will need to master the bedroom, which means becoming a pro at fully satisfying her. One of the greatest ways to encourage your Queen to explore being a sex goddess is to get her in the mood. How you can expertly help her to relax and enjoy your powers of seduction is through breast massage.

How do you give your goddess the breast massage she'll crave time and time again? Begin by sitting on your bed, then you can either have your Queen lie with her head in your lap or you will need to straddle her and have her lie back on the bed. Begin by kissing and caressing her. Then begin to cup her breasts, wrap your fingers around their fullness, and squeeze softly. Then begin to massage her breasts, slowly rotating your hands around their entire surface. Start off gently then increase intensity.

Pinching your Queen's nipples can also be arousing but do this gently. Interchange massaging with kissing her neck and stomach. Ask her how she feels. The more she sees how attentive you are, the more turned on she will be. Women need to be desired and worshipped. This is what you do when you place 100 percent of your focus on her. Stimulate her mind and her breasts by speaking softly into her ear. Let her know how good she feels in your arms. Ask her if she likes how you touch her. Ask her what she needs from you in the moment. Let her know how much you enjoy turning her on. Compliment her about her hair, skin, and body. You can also use this time to recite affirmations.

My book *Turning Point* has a complete outline of how you can incorporate them into your lovemaking. It is important to communicate with your Queen and show your appreciation for her to unleash her sex goddess. Kiss her breasts and maybe you can follow this up with oral pleasure. Moving from her breasts to her stomach and then her divine center, her vagina is the perfect way to stimulate her. As she becomes more aroused, she may wish to take the lead and get on top or do pacesetting. Show your enthusiasm for any display of dominance, because when she steps into her power as leader, she unleashes her full ability to become a Goddess of Love. It's important that your sex becomes goddess worship and you extend foreplay as long as possible.

Foreplay

Foreplay is your opportunity to ensure your goddess is fully aroused and ready to have sex. Let's face it, when she is aroused. you'll also be turned on. For women, foreplay can actually make sex more pleasurable. Foreplay can also help a couple feel closer and more intimate, which ultimately may lead you and your Queen to feel more aroused. Foreplay is really about building an emotional connection and getting some excitement going.

You can't know what your Queen likes and wants during foreplay if you don't talk about it. So ask your Queen questions about how he or she wants to be touched, stroked, kissed, and caressed.

Aim for at least 10 minutes to give your bodies enough time to warm up. What's important is to focus on kissing and stroking the stomach, inner thighs, and breasts before moving toward the genitals.

Recent studies show that women were more likely to orgasm if their man worshipped them with deep kissing, manual genital stimulation, and/or oral sex in addition to vaginal intercourse. Only 65 percent of the heterosexual women said they "usually-always" orgasmed during a sexual encounter, compared with 86 percent of lesbian women. This could mean that Queens are not getting enough foreplay. It's further evidence that lavishing your Queen with it adds up to more excitement and a sex goddess who is fully sexually satisfied.

Oral Sex

Oral sex has been around for centuries and is called by several names: cunnilingus, and slang terms like going down, going downtown, eating her out, pussy licking, sucking clam or sucking oysters, munching carpet, or perhaps some other equally ridiculous slang term commonly used to describe it. Although there are a variety of slang terms people use to describe giving oral sex pleasure to a woman, we are going to call it with the proper respect it deserves, female led oral sex.

Oral sex, to a woman, is the most important skill you will need to master if you want to call yourself a great lover. Your goddess will probably orgasm more from oral sex than when having intercourse alone, and this is a win-win situation for both of you. Part of oral sex is understanding how it relates to goddess worship and reaching the divine. It is the mental engagement and deep connection along with physical intimacy that makes female led sex so exciting and desirable. The Female Led Relationship offers the freedom to explore with consent from both of you and with lots of communication.

Even though the woman makes the rules in a Female Led Relationship, everything still requires an agreement from both of you. Women have admitted that some of the benefits are having your needs taken care of, deciding who does which chore, handling the money, and not having to ask permission for any purchase, having a greater sense of power and control than your outside life might have, and being more dominant in your sex life. Many couples in normal relationships are exploring a female led lifestyle because many men have the fantasy of serving a strong woman and being dominated by one.

In my experience, it is mostly men who first discover and want to initiate the change to female led, but once his Queen is involved, the relationship begins to evolve quickly. Men tend to take charge during work and deal with the stress of having major responsibilities. Many are happy for their woman to take the lead at home, and they simply submit to her leadership. They look forward to when their woman comes home and tells them it's time to cook dinner, rub her feet, clean the house, or give her pleasure. It's liberating to relinquish control and give in to her every desire.

If your goddess has to resort to faking orgasms or pretending to enjoy sex when she'd rather be doing anything else, this is a failure on your part and must be changed. Oral sex done properly will change your sex life, and more importantly, your woman's sex life. Ultimately, it can make you and your woman have a great love life together, and sharing love between people is what it is all about in life. Oral sex should never be faked, played, or simulated. If you don't want to give her oral sex, it's the same as her not wanting to have intercourse with you.

You may orgasm easily during sex, but most women don't. In addition, if she's not enjoying oral sex because your technique is off or you don't know what you are doing, this can be the beginning of a disaster. Unhappy wife, disastrous life. Today, it is important for men to learn how to master oral sex if they're going to keep a strong, demanding Queen happy. Bad oral sex makes a woman feel uncomfortable and makes you seem unsure of yourself. This gets you in the doghouse fast and leaves you with a raging, unhappy, unsatisfied woman.

Learning how to give proper oral sex will teach you how to truly serve your goddess and make love to her with your mouth and tongue. I will show you how to achieve a mind-blowing orgasm, which I call the cosmic orgasm. It is so powerful that you will feel like you're having an orgasm with her as she comes into your mouth. The divine oral sex I am describing can result in true joy and spiritual orgasm that will heal your soul and make you feel like the king of the world. It will be the greatest enhancement of your love life within your present relationship and will unlock a new level of passion between you and your woman.

To become an artist and deliver divine bliss to your goddess, you must be genuinely devoted to loving, obeying, and serving her and putting her pleasure first. The power of love will give you the strength, purity of heart, and connection to the feminine divine to dissolve anything and all that might still be separating you at this very moment from achieving the ultimate cosmic orgasm with your goddess.

So, take a look inside, gentleman, observe your very own present attitude and feelings toward your goddess, and make proper adjustments and give total freedom to your partner. Do you want to commit and make your partner fully happy right now? Do you want to make a genuine effort to achieve love, be obedient to her, and serve all her needs and bring her pleasure, or not? Do you want your partner to find true love and absolute long-lasting bliss and happiness in your relationship? If you want to unleash the real sex goddess, then, this is how you do it.

The Female Led Relationship offers an opportunity to explore more than just a great daily life with your Goddess of Love. It gives you a chance to improve all aspects of her life, making her a greater leader and a more confident woman and connecting to her on the deepest level possible. Oral sex is the pathway to the divine. The vagina and uterus give life, and many believe it is a connection to the spiritual realm. Why is this important? Humans are not just physical creatures. We are mental, physical, and spiritual beings, and many times unhappiness in individuals and relationships can stem from the inability to satisfy all parts.

As the man in your goddess's life, you learned it was your duty to ensure your woman feels fully served. In daily life, this is accomplished by doing everything she commands and allowing her to take control of all aspects of your life. Sex is an extremely important part of your service, and now you will be able to connect to her on levels that no one else can. In the bedroom, you will now be charged with giving your Queen the ultimate sexual experience by making the sex all about her and placing the focus on her.

By doing this, you will gain great pleasure as well. You will not only feel more satisfied in your own orgasms, but you will be confident that you are solely responsible for giving her the ultimate sexual pleasure. Oral sex becomes the center of the entire sexual session because the act is the main method most women require to climax effectively. Now you have become the most important person in her life. One of the exciting parts of a FLR is sharing as many new experiences in your daily life as possible.

Now, as a man, you are supporting your goddess on her path to connecting to the Feminine Divine, the Divine Cosmic

Force of the Universe. This divine connection will enhance your present relationship and bring new energy into your life. Tantric masters have long preached the importance of sexual energy. This is so powerful that they use it to transcend. They learn techniques to expand and deepen the orgasm experience. In female led oral sex, this is what you are doing for her.

Sex becomes the ritual you will perform throughout the entire session to help your goddess have that mind-blowing cosmic experience together with her orgasm. Your sex becomes a ceremony, a celebration of the divine. You become more connected to the universe when you bring your goddess to orgasm, and you are also experiencing euphoria. In Tantric sex, the male energy is like fire— burning hot and fast, but a woman's energy is like water—it flows. It is this difference that makes female led oral sex so much more complex. You will no longer think of your male ego or your male pleasure. You will no longer receive oral sex or a blow job unless your goddess desires it for her own reasons. You will now live to bring pleasure to your goddess first.

Once her needs are fulfilled, then you can fulfill yours. That is the power of FLR. Once you fully commit to satisfying your goddess, you will receive a tremendous energy boost and strengthening of your worship of your Queen. I recommend performing oral sex on your woman as often as she will allow. Personally, I demand daily oral worship and praise of me as the goddess. I see it as very crucial to my overall well-being. Oral sex changes a woman's eagerness for sex because she knows it's for her pleasure.

How can you resist someone who wants to worship you? I feel that one of the greatest ways to show your devotion is to serve your woman's every desire, and this includes every sexual desire. It is important that you make her feel truly adored and worshipped during sex. You must allow her the time to relax and forget about all of the stresses of life. This is her moment of fantasy and adventure. Take her to another place with sex that fulfills her to the core.

Connecting to your goddess's divine through the vagina helps to strengthen the relationship among many other health benefits. First, when you make sex about lovemaking and worship, orgasms are much easier to achieve, and they raise oxytocin which helps to combat stress and regulate cortisol in the body. People sleep better, regulate appetite and hormones, and report feeling happy and positive. So when you focus on your goddess's pleasure, you are improving all facets of her being. You are ensuring that all aspects of her life are fulfilled.

Connecting to the divine through sex improves your spiritual connection, which is the most powerful way to be connected. I feel that today, this is the missing link. People have become very dissatisfied with religions and many belief systems, and I believe that this is because we were constantly looking for pastors, priests, or churches to create happiness in our lives. The spiritual connection to the universe, divine, and God lies within us, so as partners in a union, the responsibility is on you and your Queen to create the happiness you are seeking through the daily activities in your relationship. This is what makes female led so special. The feminine represents Mother Earth. This is one of the greatest powers in the universe. When you unleash this power in your goddess, you open up pathways to improve your lives exponentially because both male and female energy are released.

Einstein said, "Energy can neither be created nor destroyed." This means that energy is a real and powerful force, ever present. There are some practitioners who believe that we can manifest ourselves through the use of sexual energy. This is part of Tantra teachings, and it is believed that through the harnessing of sexual energy, it is possible to achieve enlightenment. But traditional intercourse where the focus is on the man is much more about releasing energy than building it and harnessing. This can only happen through the worship of the woman through oral sex and in so doing prolonging the experience, which then takes both you and your Queen to higher levels.

CHAPTER 14

Sex Is for Goddess Pleasure

The first rule of Female Led Relationship is that sex is for the Queen's pleasure, and now as part of goddess worship, sex is for your goddess's pleasure. You need to give her more pleasure than she has ever experienced. For hundreds of years, women have had to focus on men's sexual pleasure and settled for mediocre or no enjoyment in the process. Oral sex for women was a fun pastime that some lucky couples experienced but most women and men were unaware of how to navigate the female divine center, the vagina.

I was once horrified to learn how many women never allow a man to see them fully nude in the light or covered up under blankets. In a Female Led Relationship, a woman's entire body, including her vagina, must be worshipped by men. You will need to learn how to get your goddess so relaxed that she willingly allows you to explore her body and learn everything you can about her vagina.

Becoming a master of oral sex will be how you, her submissive supportive gentleman demonstrates your ultimate devotion to your goddess through proper goddess worship. Oral sex must be enacted like a ceremony. One of the big things missing in sex lives is the idea of ceremony. Lingerie, candles, satin sheets are all part of the ceremony. Female-led women generally know that the ceremony of sex is very important and it's the little things that add up to a fantastic experience. So as the Queen's servant and the man, you will need to prepare for the ceremony of oral sex. Get a nice big pillow you reserve only for sex, get a fun wedge to put her hips up on, candles, massage oils — anything you can to make the space special. Buy her sexy underwear that you'll want to feel before you begin and see her walking around in.

You need to partake in ensuring sex a special experience. Reading this book is a great start because you will be able to delight her when you can show off your oral skills. Don't feel bad if you have all these questions in your head: "Does my woman's vagina look like a mystery down there?" "What the heck do I do?" "Where do I begin?" "What's the best area to focus on?" It can be confusing. There are inner and outer flaps and folds of skin and maybe some hair, then even more folds and more flaps, and the flower, the bud of the clitoris. "Do I lick, kiss; rough, soft, teasing?" You will have a million questions, and I will do my best to answer them all. But remember, this one guiding principle — it all works, and you need to gauge how your Queen is turned on by it. You need to become very tuned into how she is feeling.

I am amazed at how many couples never discuss sex. After a sex session, it is mandatory to ask what worked, what she liked and did not like. During sex, it is fun to ask, "You like that?" "How does that feel?" These are the conversations to have, not just random, "Ooh, babe, I like that," or "Hit it hard." The worst is when men feel the need to talk all the way through. There is a time and place. Oral sex is a time when your woman wants to be relaxed and you are modifying your technique to learn what works for her. It's not a session you are trying to get through so you can get to intercourse. You will approach oral sex like it's the main course, not the appetizer. We savor the main course in a meal like it's the best food we have ever had, and this is the approach you take when performing oral sex.

One of the most important things to do with sex is to get your goddess in the mood. Too many men underestimate the importance of this. If your Queen is stressed from the day, the first thing you want to do is get her to relax. This is the lead-up. Take over the chores—cooking dinner, washing the dishes, or other chores. Surprise her by drawing her a nice bath or giving her a massage. Let her unwind by discussing anything she wants to talk about. When she is relaxed, she is more likely to entertain having sex. Surprises are a great way to show a woman you really care and you are really interested in fulfilling her needs.

In the past, I cannot recall one time when my partners, even in long-term relationships, brought me flowers or some other gift for no reason. Today, this happens almost every day, without me ever having to mention it. So, when you are trying to seduce your goddess, do the unexpected. When you are finally in bed ready to have sex, begin slowly and gently. Make sure she is in a comfortable position. Tell her you are going to be switching it up if you have not had oral sex for a long time. Get her in the mood first. I cannot stress the importance of this. Kiss her neck, her lips, her breasts, her chest, and her navel, making your way down. Savor each moment as though you are discovering her body for the first time. Tell her how beautiful she is, how much you love the feel of her curves and her skin. It's going to be so much more soothing when you keep the focus on your Queen at all times. Men often underestimate the power of a compliment. Now you are going to be performing oral sex like there is a real art to it.

While you are performing oral sex, you may have a lot of thoughts going through your mind. You may wonder, "Is she enjoying it?" "Am I doing this correctly?" Be confident and look for clues. Is she relaxed? Is she moaning? Is she smiling? If she isn't, ask questions: "How is this?" "Do you like this?" In the beginning, it should be much more like you are teasing her. You're getting her excited. You're kissing outside her panties, then slowly slipping them off. Maintaining eye contact. Every movement and eye contact should be deliberate. You're watching her breathing, her noises, the look on her face. You are maintaining all the focus on her enjoyment. The idea is to slowly seduce her as you are getting her excited.

Now you are ready to give mind-blowing oral sex to your Queen. Your focus should always be on how you can connect to the divine force and energy in her, how you can get her to come alive. Every goddess loves oral sex and enjoys it repeatedly. In fact, there are very few Queens on the planet who don't grow to absolutely enjoy oral sex done right. You are now challenged to become a master of giving it. You will be rewarded with a happy partner who will be so much more enthusiastic about sex. When men are able to fully satisfy a goddess, relationships become exciting and adventurous.

CHAPTER 15

How to Perform Goddess Worship

When you are finally in bed ready to have sex, begin slowly and gently. Make sure she is in a comfortable position. Tell her you will be switching it up if you have not had oral sex for a long time. Get her in the mood first. I cannot stress the importance of this. Kiss her neck, her lips, her breasts, her chest, and her navel, making your way down. Savor each moment as though you are discovering her body for the first time. Tell her how beautiful she is, how much you love the feel of her curves and her skin. Men often underestimate the power of a compliment. It's going to be so much more soothing when you keep the focus on your Queen at all times. Now you are going to be performing oral sex like there is a real art to it.

Now you are ready to give mind-blowing oral sex to your Queen. Your focus should always be on how you can connect to the divine force and energy in her, how you can get her to come alive. One of the worst experiences I had with a man was regarding his wife, a gorgeous model, who lay on the bed, not making any sound or movement while he performed sex acts. I saw this as a huge problem, and I suggested that he needed to talk with her. You need to have open communication and feedback from your goddess. If you cannot determine if she enjoys the sex or how she feels, you will need to request feedback directly. It's the only way you will learn and improve your skills.

One of the most important parts of foreplay is to place your goddess in a relaxed, happy mood. Women can be apprehensive if they are new to oral pleasure and positive compliments help reassure her that you are eager and excited to please her. The idea is you want to encourage her to enjoy becoming a sex goddess and receiving pleasure. You must make her feel happy, confident, and aroused. Tell her that her scent is provocative and turns you on. Once you get down there, stop for a moment and tell her that you love the way she tastes. Compliment that her pussy is fantastic, powerful, and you love everything about it. If you can convey each of these beliefs to her in a sincere way, you're going to be on your way to giving head and getting ahead.

Once you get down there, taking your time is another great way to help her feel more relaxed and excited about what you have in store for her. Begin slowly. Caress, massage, kiss, and draw out the initial contact. This is the foreplay. You want to ensure she is really in the mood. Too many men cut this short and get down to the vagina too fast. Women will never enjoy oral sex if the foreplay is rushed. Many times, this is the problem with intercourse. The foreplay is rushed, and she doesn't have time to relax, then it's "wham bam, thank you, ma'am." This is forbidden in oral sex. You need to give her time to build her divine energy, and you almost need to be going into your own state of euphoria as you get down to performing your mind-blowing oral sex on her.

After complimenting her, move slowly down her stomach and thigh. Take your time kissing, hugging, touching, and even talking a little bit more about how going down on her has been a fantasy of yours and you're really excited. Make sure she's aroused before you dive in between her legs. Once you're down there, continue taking your time and start with light licks from the bottom of her pussy to the top. The clitoris is extremely sensitive, so you don't want to dive in right away. The reason why oral sex is so powerful is the clitoris, which is the most nerve-rich part of a woman's body and is the main region of focus of oral sex for her, but you want to take your time getting there.. The clitoral glans contain about eight thousand nerve endings, making it the powerhouse of pleasure.

To get some perspective, that's twice as many nerve endings as the penis. And its potential doesn't end there. This tiny erogenous zone spreads to fifteen thousand other nerves in the vagina area, which explains why women love oral sex so much. We know women are all unique, and the pussy is not any different, so every woman's pussy and even their clits are different. Every woman needs a different kind of stimulation to feel satisfied, depending on her unique biology. For some women, it's so sensitive that they may not want it to be stimulated directly. Some women may prefer touching near and around the clitoris but not directly on it because it is simply too sensitive with direct stimulation. Other women are fine with direct stimulation and even want you to suck on it until they orgasm.

Oh, and one more thing, we've all heard about the infamous G-spot. Maybe you've been confused about where it is or how to find it. This notorious pleasure zone became sensationalized back in the eighties when it was believed that if you could only access the G-spot inside the vagina, it would promote female orgasm. But now we know that some women have more sensitivity from the internal parts of the clitoral complex. That's why some women prefer vaginal penetration and intercourse more than other women. It may take a bit of time for you to learn how to stimulate all the right areas, but with practice comes perfection, which is why it is important to have regular sex and engage in oral sex with your goddess as the focus. Anyone can slip the penis in and move back and forth until you orgasm. It takes a real Casanova to master giving great oral sex to a Queen.

There is also the opportunity to add sex toys. These can add lots of variation and excitement. The following are the best sex toys available for her. Vibrators are probably the most common type of sex toy. Wand vibrators are more intense with higher RPM. They can also be great massagers for the shoulders, legs, and back. Clitoral vibrators are typically much smaller and are best for people who like direct clitoral stimulation.

Dildos are meant to simulate penile penetration. They can be any length or girth. There are ones that are two inches and ones that are monster-sized. People who enjoy the feeling of being penetrated or like the feeling of fullness in their vagina or anus might enjoy dildo play.

Butt plugs stimulate the ring of nerves around the anus. The difference between using a butt plug and using a dildo is where a dildo goes in and out, the butt plug just stays in and gives a sustained feeling of fullness. The rabbit toy is a combo of an external vibrator and a G-spot toy. It has an external part that usually looks like rabbit ears that provides vibration to the clitoris. And a second attachment goes inside the vagina for G-spot stimulation, so you get double the sensation. Anal beads are another interesting toy.

Unlike butt plugs, which typically go in and stay in, anal beads provide the sensation of the anal sphincter opening and closing. Pulling them out as you orgasm can create a more intense orgasm.

Be careful when using sex toys, though. Master your technique of oral first, and then add them in as a side dish. Make sure you don't upset the whole experience by trying to make the sex toy the focus and make sure she is comfortable with the use of the toy. As with everything, personal hygiene and cleaning of sex toys directly after use are recommended.

CHAPTER 16

Sexual Techniques to Unlock Her Sex Goddess

What are some of the best sexual techniques to help your Queen unlock her sex goddess? Her transition to sex goddess comes during your journey through goddess worship and switching things up will be very important. There should be no rules or normal patterns when embarking on this adventure. Try some ways to change your mindset about sex and make it an opportunity to learn about each other and become deeply connected.

Here are some tips:

1. Practice eroticism which is the practice of slowing down, focusing our awareness, and deepening your appreciation for your Queen and your opportunity to serve and worship her.

2. Care for Your Body. You've likely heard that phrase "your body is your temple." Though according to ancient wisdom traditions like Ayurveda or Tantra, you really are divine and your body is holy. It's both

your sanctuary and vehicle while you're here in this human form. With that in mind, consider how you and your Queen care for your bodies.

3. Create a Ritual. A ritual is an activity or action that we perform to connect with the divine. If your body is a temple, consider sex with your partner or by yourself a ritual. It's an act of worship. Make your worship an offering to the divine. You can add elements such as candles, music, and incense. Sexual energy is the merging of our human form with pure consciousness or the divine. Sex as a ritual has long been performed to release fertile energy to the earth to encourage crops to grow. What is the energy you want to release?

4. Meditate on Pleasure. Consider sex a meditation—an awareness of pleasure meditation. Rather than focusing on achieving orgasm, can you focus on giving and receiving pleasure with presence? Experiment with touch. Communicate with your Queen about what turns you both on. Look into each other's eyes. While experiencing pleasure in a particular spot in the body, see if you can grow it throughout your body and all the way to the crown of your head. Sex allows us to create a connection with another that builds trust and intimacy and, lastly, brings us closer to the divine. It helps raise our energy, elevate our mood, and gives us a more positive outlook on life.

Focus on Stimulating Erogenous Zones

There are other body parts other than main sexual organs that can really turn on your goddess. These include feet, scalp, ears, lips, naval, fingertips, arms, thighs, chest, behind the knees, abs, nape of neck, ears, back of neck, inner thigh, stomach, and tailbone. Focusing on stimulating these and other parts of the body altogether can dramatically enhance your goddess's sexual pleasure.

Queening

Encourage your Queen to take the lead, and one of the best ways to do this is Queening. Queening involves your Queen straddling your face for oral pleasure. It's an ancient art in which a woman presses and rubs her genitalia and/or anus against the tongue, lips, and nose of her subordinate. She classically positions herself in a sitting on or over your face. Some couples use the Queening stool which makes it easier to assume this position.

One of the wonderful ways to help your Queen to become a sex goddess is to build her confidence by supporting her efforts to be dominant. Queening offers this opportunity, and many women enjoy the position as they are indeed on top. Literally. Facesitting is common among dominant and submissive individuals, for demonstrating superiority and for sexual gratification. The full-weight body pressure, smothering, moisture, body odors, and darkness can be perceived as powerful sexual attractions or compulsions. You want to encourage your Queen to feel power during sex in any way possible. This is guaranteed to assist her in her transformation into sex goddess.

Sexual Grounding

Sexual grounding refers to the practice of being present and aware of one's physical and emotional state during sexual activity. Sexual grounding is important in goddess sex worship because it helps create an atmosphere of presence and connection between all participants. Being present in the moment allows a sacred space to be created so that participants can truly honor the energies of the Divine Feminine. By being present, one can open up to the power of connection and pleasure that is available through the experience.

Sexual grounding refers to the practice of being present and aware of one's physical and emotional state during sexual activity. It can involve focusing on physical sensations in the body, being aware of one's breath, and being mindful of one's thoughts and feelings. The goal of sexual grounding is to increase pleasure, intimacy, and to be more present during the sexual experience.

This technique can be achieved by various methods such as:

- Breathing techniques: Focusing on the breath can help bring awareness to the present moment and to release tension in the body.

- Mindfulness meditation: This can be useful to be more present during the sexual experience and to become more aware of one's physical sensations.

- Body scanning: This is a technique that consists of systematically moving attention through different parts of the body and noticing any sensations or emotions that arise.

Sexual grounding can be useful in increasing pleasure and intimacy during sexual activity, and also can be useful in addressing some sexual dysfunctions such as premature ejaculation and addressing some emotional and psychological issues related to sexual experiences.

Sexual grounding is not a magic solution and requires practice and patience. You must communicate with your partner about what you're doing and respect their boundaries and feelings. Additionally, it's important to remember that sexual grounding is not the only way to improve sexual experiences, and that other techniques such as communication, consent, and intimacy, among others, also play an essential role.

Sexual Layering

Sexual layering refers to the practice of building pleasure and intensity gradually through different types of sexual stimulation, rather than focusing on a single type of stimulation. This can include a combination of various types of physical touch, such as kissing, massaging, and stroking, as well as different types of mental and emotional stimulation, such as verbal communication, role-playing, and fantasy.

The idea behind sexual layering is that by gradually building pleasure and intensity, the sexual experience becomes more intense and satisfying. It also allows for a more varied and dynamic sexual experience, rather than focusing solely on one type of stimulation.

Examples of sexual layering techniques include:

125

- Building arousal through kissing and touching before engaging in intercourse

- Using different types of touch, such as gentle and firm strokes, to vary the intensity of the experience

- Incorporating different types of stimulation, such as oral sex, manual stimulation, and intercourse, to create a more dynamic experience

Sexual layering is not a one-size-fits-all approach and what works for one person may not work for another. Additionally, you must communicate openly and honestly with your partner about your desires and boundaries, and be aware of their needs and desires as well. It's also important to remember that sexual layering is not the only way to improve sexual experiences, and that other techniques, such as communication, consent, intimacy, and self-exploration also play an important role.

Nipple Orgasms

If you want to successfully turn your goddess into the ultimate sex goddess, then you need to really turn her on. All the fun begins early on so before you begin to worship her divine center, get her warmed up with some nipple play and maybe even achieve nipple orgasm.

The idea of reaching climax without going near your Queen's genitals might seem far-fetched, but plenty of couples have successfully achieved a nipple orgasm. Orgasms are neuropsychological responses.

They are byproducts of built-up sexual tension and stimulation, paired with neuropsychological discharges.

Stimulation of the nipples can lead to this kind of tension build-up in the body, resulting in orgasm.

In short, a nipple orgasm is when you reach a sexual climax only from stimulating the nipples or surrounding breast area without any clitoral or vaginal stimulation.

Nipples are major erogenous zones, with lots of nerve endings to provide intense sensations. Many people report that this type of climax feels similar to a pelvic-related orgasm. When our primary erogenous zones like the nipples, neck, and feet are stimulated, they can cause a sexual response. This is due to the sensory cortex in the brain. Our brains and bodies are interconnected in a network of nerve-endings, sending signals back and forth through the spine. When your Queen's nipples are stimulated, a signal is sent to the brain letting it know it feels good. The brain registers this stimulation as sexual, sending a corresponding signal to the genitals. That's right, the same area of the brain that lights up when we have our genitals stimulated lights up when we have our nipples stimulated.

Your Queen's nipples are by far the most sensitive part of her entire breast region. A high volume of nerve endings is responsible for these intense erotic sensations.

Start by experimenting with different touching techniques. Focus on her breathing and help her to release any stress or tension. You want to put your Queen into a relaxing almost meditative state.

Once you're both mentally ready, use a light touch to circle her entire breast area, slowly making your way toward the nipple. Trace over her nipples with a single finger, and slowly rub in different directions. You could incorporate a soft feather tickler toy or ice cubes to experiment with temperature.

By this time, her nipples are likely to be erect, helping further build anticipation and enhance sensation. If she's ready, you can experiment with pinching and/or twisting.

A nipple-focused massage is one of the most effective, powerful methods of achieving an orgasm of this kind. Research confirms that stimulating the breasts, chest, and nipples specifically can lead to sexual pleasure and an orgasm.

Start slowly, and gently increase the intensity to generate tension and anticipation. Slowly begin stroking your hips, stomach, and neck, using massage oil if you want. Once you feel she is sufficiently aroused, begin circling her breasts and gently apply a squeezing motion. Avoid directly touching your nipples at this point, solely focusing on her breasts. You can continue to massage other areas of her body as well.

The key at this phase is to build anticipation, bringing her body to a stage where she is completely aroused and ready for more. But practice a bit of edging technique where you back off the pressure then add more. Denying or delaying her pleasure can increase anticipation and make the final result even more powerful. You are building up her energy before you move to her divine center and really give her mind-blowing orgasms.

You can continue circling her breasts to maintain tension, and slowly begin pinching her nipples if you want. This pinching action can help release oxytocin. You can also experiment with what's known as the "rolling technique." Instead of direct pinching, grip the nipple base and slowly roll it between your index finger and thumb. This can provide an all-over wave of sensation for your goddess, especially when combined with slick massage oil.

When you focus on your Queen's nipples, stimulating them with fingers, toys, or a mouth, you can create a strong enough arousal response to produce an orgasm, even before oral worship or penetration. The nipple massage is a great way to extend your goddess worship and even turn your entire sex routine into a full body arousal ritual.

Learn the Signs of Arousal

It is important to begin to learn the signs of arousal in a woman and, more precisely, *your* woman. All women are going to have their own unique signals. These are signs that will help in beginning to gauge your Queens arousal:

- **Lubrication**

Let's begin with one of the most obvious signs of arousal in women—lubrication. The woman's body will begin to excrete lubricant when she is ready to be penetrated. If you touch your woman's pussy and it is dry, then it is likely she is not aroused enough for penetration. Occasionally, there can be medical issues that create a lack of lubrication, and this is more commonly seen in older women. However, as a general rule, I tell clients that if you need lubricants for vaginal penetration at the beginning of sex, then the woman is not aroused enough and more foreplay needs to happen. Lubricants are great for things such as anal sex, or if you have intercourse for hours. Even then, it is important to pay attention to how naturally lubricated your woman is in the process.

• Skin Changes

This can be a fun one to notice in different partners. At times, you can see physical changes in your woman's skin such as goosebumps that can extend to her arms, legs, stomach, and buttocks. Another noticeable skin change is flushing in the chest and face. As the woman's heart rate increases, more blood flow will be present throughout the body, so you may feel more heat radiating from the skin in places such as the breasts, pussy, and upper legs.

• Breath

When we are in a deep state of arousal, our breathing will naturally change and become shorter and heavier. If your woman has been trained in Tantric breathing, she may have a deeper fuller breath, but you still will be able to notice slight changes in her breathing.

• Verbalizations

This one can be complicated. Currently we live in a world where so many women are shut down in various ways, and that includes verbalizing during sex. If the throat chakra is blocked, then she is going to have a hard time letting noise escape during sex or directly asking for what she wants. Thankfully, other women are perfectly comfortable allowing their voices to be heard so, again, pay attention to the nuances. When you begin to hear small gasps, moans, grunts — hell, even screams—then you know you are on the right track. Sometimes the verbalizations will become more breathy as she gets into a deeper state of arousal.

Side note: Women, *don't fake it!* When you do this, you only confuse your guy and create distance in the sexual relationship. If you are not feeling it, have the guts to own that something isn't working or that you may not be in a mental state to allow an orgasm. The worst thing you can do is to pretend.

• Body Movements

These are great indicators of arousal, or when something isn't working. There are a multitude of different body movements that can be watched, so this aspect is simply about being observant. An example of a positive body movement would be slight tremors in the hands, feet, belly, and chest that indicate orgasmic energy. If you see any buckling of hips, then this can indicate that the woman wants more. Some indications of things not working would be if your woman looks like a dead body and is simply lying there, if she is pulling away from you when you are trying to penetrate, or if her hips appear frozen. Another one that is often missed is when women are slightly pushing away with their hands.

I was with a lover who wasn't doing anything wrong, and I was indeed turned on, but I was feeling a bit uncertain about the positioning. He noticed that every time he thrust into me, my thighs would tense, so he brought it to my attention and asked if everything was all right. I hadn't noticed that my legs were tensing, so we changed positions and moved on to a wonderful round of sexing. Observe what is happening and ask your partner if they need an adjustment.

• Vaginal Changes

Listen to your Queen's pussy. I know, it seems like common sense, but it's often something that is overlooked. If you are noticing not only color and lubrication changes, but also your women's vaginal canal expanding, then arousal is increasing. If you feel or see muscle ripples, that is usually another sign that things are moving in the right direction. In orgasm, a woman's pussy will internally feel like ocean waves as the ripples move down the vaginal canal.

Multiple Orgasms

Multiple orgasms refer to the ability to experience more than one orgasm during a sexual encounter or in a short period of time. Here are some tips to help increase the chances of having multiple orgasms:

- Understand her body: Knowing her sexual response cycle and what type of touch or stimulation feels good to her is important in being able to achieve multiple orgasms.

- Practice Kegel exercises: These exercises help to strengthen the pelvic floor muscles, which can improve sexual response and increase the chances of having multiple orgasms.Encourage your goddess to do them on a regular basis.

- Engage in non-intercourse activities: Engaging in activities such as oral sex, manual stimulation, or the use of sex toys can increase the chances of having multiple orgasms.

- Experiment with different types of stimulation: Experimenting with different types of touch, such as light and gentle vs. firm and intense, can lead to different types of orgasms.

- Communicate with your goddess: Communicating with your goddess about both or your desires and what feels good to you can help to increase the chances of having multiple orgasms.

- Stay relaxed and reduce stress: Stress and tension can inhibit orgasm and reduce sexual response, so it's important to stay relaxed and reduce stress levels as much as possible.

It's important to remember achieving multiple orgasms takes practice and experimentation. In addition, the goal of goddess is not always to orgasm. Connection, pleasure, and intimacy are crucial.

Sexual Rocking

Sexual rocking and swaying refer to the rhythmic movement of the body during sexual activity to enhance pleasure and intimacy. Sexual rocking refers to a back-and-forth movement of the hips, while sexual swaying refers to a side-to-side movement of the hips. Both techniques can be used during intercourse, manual stimulation, or oral sex, and they can be used to create different types of sensation and to increase pleasure.

These techniques can also be used in conjunction with other techniques, such as sexual layering, edging, and peaking, to create a more dynamic and intense sexual experience.

It's important to communicate with your partner and pay attention to their cues and signals to ensure that the rocking and swaying movements are pleasurable for both partners. Additionally, it's important to note that not everyone may be comfortable with these techniques and it's important to respect your partner's boundaries and preferences.

It's also important to remember that sexual rocking and swaying is not the only way to improve sexual experiences, and that other techniques such as communication, consent, intimacy, and self-exploration also play an important role.

Angling

Sexual angling is important in goddess sex worship because the basic premise of goddess sex is the acknowledgement of the Divine Feminine and the acknowledgment of each partner in the ritual. Like rocking, angling is a form of intentional, sensual movement between partners that deepens connection, activates energies, and opens the spiritual pathways to the Divine Feminine.

This practice allows each partner to become a part of a union that is more than physical, more than mental—a union that transcends time and space and allows for a deeper understanding of the Divine Feminine. Through angling, each partner can open to the ancient wisdom that lies within and tap into the energy of the goddess to experience a higher form of pleasure.

Angling during sexual activity refers to adjusting the angle of the pelvis in order to increase pleasure and to maximize the stimulation of certain areas of the genitals. This technique can be particularly helpful for the female partner to leverage her pelvic floor muscles and to increase the chances of orgasm. By angling the pelvis in different ways, women can change the angle of penetration and the amount of pressure on the clitoris, which can lead to better orgasms.

Angling refers to adjusting the angle of the pelvis to increase pleasure and maximize the stimulation of certain areas of the genitals. This technique can be particularly helpful for her to leverage her pelvic floor muscles and increase the chances of orgasm.

By angling the pelvis in different ways, women can change the angle of penetration and the amount of pressure on the clitoris, which can lead to different types of orgasm.

It's important to communicate with your partner and to pay attention to their cues and signals to ensure that the angling movements are pleasurable for both partners. Additionally, it's important to note that not everyone may be comfortable with this technique and it's important to respect your partner's boundaries and preferences.

It's also important to remember that sexual angling is not the only way to improve sexual experiences, and that other techniques such as communication, consent, intimacy, and self-exploration also play an important role.

Sexual Levering

Sexual leveraging is important in goddess sex worship because it allows for a deeper level of connection and opens up the receiving partner to the Divine Feminine. Through leveraging, each partner can arch their body and use their posture to allow the Divine Feminine energies to move freely between them. This practice encourages deeper pleasure and connection in that it emphasizes the need for both partners to be aware and in tune with each other during the ritual. Levering allows for a deeper understanding of the partner and a heightened experience of the Divine Feminine energies. This gives the partners a better foundation to build a deeper spiritual connection and cultivate a stronger intimacy between them.

Sexual levering around the corner and against the vaginal walls refers to the practice of using different angles and positions during sexual activity to stimulate different areas of the vagina.

Sexual levering around the corner refers to angling the penis or sex toy at a specific angle in order to stimulate the front or back wall of the vagina, which can lead to different types of orgasm.

Sexual levering against the vaginal walls refers to using a specific position or angle during penetration to apply pressure against the walls of the vagina, which can lead to different types of sensation.

It's important for you and your Queen to communicate and pay attention to cues and signals to ensure that the levering movements are pleasurable for both of you.

Additionally, it's important to note that not everyone may be comfortable with this technique and it's important to respect your Queen's boundaries and preferences. It's also important to remember that sexual levering is not the only way to improve sexual experiences, and that other techniques such as communication, consent, intimacy, and self-exploration also play an important role. It's also important to note that some positions might not be comfortable for everyone, especially if there are any physical limitations and to be aware of this and to find the positions that work best for you and your partner.

Best Moves during Vagina Penetration

These were specific sexual moves and methods that women reported gave them the most pleasure:

- **Angling.** Rotating, raising, or lowering pelvis and hips during penetration to adjust where inside the vagina the toy or penis rubs.

- **Pairing.** You stimulate her clitoris with a finger or sex toy simultaneously with penetration.

- **Rocking.** The base of a penis or sex toy rubs against the clitoris constantly during penetration by staying all the way inside the vagina rather than thrusting in and out. Usually used when the woman is on top.

- **Shallowing.** Penetrative touch just inside the entrance of the vagina. Women reported having really amazing sex with penetration just going in an inch.

Best Sex Toys

Sex toys are important in goddess sex worship because they can be used to explore different sensations, levels of pleasure, and pathways of energy exchange. For example, the use of sex toys can help the partners access states of ecstatic and powerful arousal, as well as facilitate a deeper connection to the Divine Feminine energies. Sex toys can also provide a safe place to explore their own boundaries, which is an important part of learning to worship the goddess and surrender to her power.

Additionally, sexual energy toys provide a space for celebration and honoring of the goddess, through pleasurable and passionate activity. Ultimately, sex toys can help to open up both partners to new heights of connection and pleasure, ultimately allowing for a deeper spiritual practice with the goddess.

The best sex toys found to give the most pleasure are:

For angling. Sex swings allow the woman to rotate, raise, or lower her pelvis on the penetration item to allow for maximum pleasure.

For pairing. A silicone mini finger vibrator stimulates your clitoris during penetration; a strap-on face dildo allows your partner to penetrate you while also using their tongue to stimulate the clitoris.

For rocking. A raised ribbed "cock" sleeve with a clitoral stimulator and vibrator works for both parties: It helps thicken and support the penis for more firm erections, and the female partner can rub herself against the clitoral stimulator while being penetrated. A vibrating clitoral stimulator also delivers direct stimulation.

For shallowing. Vibrating balls or eggs are inserted just inside the vagina without the need for deep penetration.

CHAPTER 17

Sexual Energy Transmutation

Many believe sexual energy is like creative energy, which can be channeled and transformed to be a positive force and to help us in other areas of our life. Sex can transform the body, mind, and spirit and bring about new life. This transformation is called sexual transmutation. Sexual transmutation is taking the sexual energy that's building inside you and channeling it into something else. You allow the energy to build up and you purposely don't release it during sex. You could, of course, channel it directly into physical sex, as so many do, but if you need a little extra oomph of creative energy or physical might, holding off on the sex and using that energy elsewhere is the idea of sexual transmutation.

Sexual energy transmutation is much like Tantric sex, which is also all about sexual energy and sacred sexuality. Ultimately, sexual transmutation is about keeping the power of that energy that's building and rising.

Sexual transmutation requires a great deal of awareness, particularly of your own sexual energy. You and your Queen are physically aware of that build of energy. During your sex sessions, you work on meditating and thinking about the sexual energy flowing through your Queen's heart to your genitals and back up. Making love is all about the exchange of energy. The more one learns about various types of energy flows at play, the deeper you can go into the sacred art of lovemaking.

Positive sexual energy balances masculine and feminine energy. Transferring these energies or experiencing these energies during sex can help balance out your physical, mental, and emotional stress that may plague you on a regular basis.

It goes deeper into the spiritual aspects of climax to explain how one can reach a sense of knowing. For those who are spiritual, it is not uncommon to access enlightenment during orgasm because of the incredible exchange of sexual energy that your body ensues.

The key is to start to understand the flow of energy that is happening in the body, how to reset that energy, when to relax, and when to take action. When you're aware of your optimum energy frequency and can access it, you're tapping into a superpower because energy is power.

All throughout your day, whether you are aware of it or not, there are energetic windows that are opening and closing. As we move through our day, we send energy into the world, and we receive energy back. Our minds, bodies and spirits are composed of energy, which vibrates out and is felt by others. Those vibrations resonate within us and impact our own energy stores.

This is why we may feel warm, calm, and cheerful in the presence of some people, but cold, anxious, and blue around others. We carry that energy with us, which impacts not only us but all the other people we come in contact with. Good energy can boost our feelings of well-being, dissolve feelings of anxiety, and improve communication. Bad energy results in feelings of discord, conflict, and resentment. Your goal should be to attract good energy and reject the bad. You can do this by raising your energy level and aligning yourself with positive vibrations.

Sexual manifesting can be used to help you and your Queen manifest great things in your life. You both can use that energy exchange to have the lives you truly desire. The harnessing of sexual energy permeates all other aspects of life and leads to the happiness that FLR couples experience.

The most powerful and energetic space is the multidimensional sexual experience. It's extremely vital before entering into a sexual experience to set the intention of what you both want to manifest from the experience. This is what makes having sex a very intimate bonding experience.

Before exchanging the physical energy, determine what you want on the emotional, energetic, and spiritual levels of the sexual connection and it will manifest. Your sexual desires, orgasm, and attraction to others are all-powerful forces. That energy can be redirected to non-sexual desires, though! This is the premise behind sexual transmutation — you take all of that sexual energy, and you focus it elsewhere.

Now you and your Queen are using sexual energy for a higher purpose in your life. Remember universal laws. Everything is connected. So, the energy you and your Queen are creating is moving outward into the world and affecting all who come into contact with you. Every living organism, every inanimate object, thought, feeling, and desire has a unique vibration unto itself. Law of Attraction states that vibrations with the same frequency are drawn to each other. Higher frequency thoughts attract more of the same just as lower frequency thoughts attract more of the same.

When you and your Queen are projecting happiness, you are automatically attracting other couples and people with a similar frequency, reining the vibration and attracting more positivity into your life. You are a magnet, and your experiences are manifestations of the energy that you give off—either consciously or subconsciously. Law of relativity reminds us that experiences on their own are not good or bad; they are neutral. It is our human perception emotion, thought, judgment that evaluate experiences and label them positive or negative. Be open about your experiences, especially in your relationship or marriage.

CHAPTER 18

Sex Magic

Sex magic harnesses the chronically suppressed power of female sexual energy to "manifest" an intention. It's a kind of modern witchcraft, but there are no pointy hats, layers of black lace, or broomsticks involved. Your intention is like a spell, and your body like the cauldron. Your Queen uses her "yonic" powers or vagina powers to bring about cosmic change. Here are the basic steps to follow:

- Before engaging in sex, decide on a "telos," an objective, feeling, or intention you intend to bring about. Choose only one objective at a time, so you can direct your undivided attention toward it.

- If you are working with a partner, discuss your telos in advance, and make sure everybody agrees on the result you intend to generate. If each of you has a different agenda, the outcome you produce will likely be garbled. Your conflicting intentions might even block or neutralize one another's—neither of you will get what you want.

- You may want to create a picture to represent your telos. Images can generate results even more effectively than words. Set a sacred space — either by lighting a candle, burning incense and/or an invocation of intention.

- Slow down. Many of us tend to rush toward the finish line, rather than pacing ourselves during sex. But drawing out the experience and allowing your sexual energy to build gradually enhances your magical power. Luxuriate in your sensuality. Let your excitement slowly increase until you feel almost ready to orgasm. Then back off. Do some deep breathing. Shift from genital stimulation to stroking other parts of the body: arms, back, feet, and so on. When the immediacy has subsided, gradually elevate the level of excitation until, once again, you almost reach the point of no return. Ease off again. Continue in the manner for as long as you like, slowly and steadily building intensity. With practice, you'll learn to "stay on the edge" for an extended period of time.

- During this period of high arousal, keep your telos in mind. The more intense your feelings, the faster you can attract what you desire, and in this near-orgasmic state your magnetic power is tremendous. You don't have to focus keenly on your objective all the time but remain aware of your purpose for engaging in this sexual ritual. As you raise energy and cycle it through your body, mentally attach your intention to that energy.

When you're finally ready to release the energy you've built up, hold your telos clearly in your mind and feel the pleasure of having your desired outcome manifested in your life. Then let your orgasm wash through you. As it does, it sweeps your intention before it, like a wave pushing a boat along its crest. The momentum you've generated carries your telos out into the universe, where it lodges in the fertile womb of the matrix and creates a magical child. After orgasm, relax and stop thinking about your telos. Enjoy the calm after the tempest. Allow the universe to do its part now.

CHAPTER 19

The Importance of Sexual Satisfaction

The importance of sexual satisfaction in a healthy, romantic Female Led Relationship is clear. Sexual satisfaction promotes relationship satisfaction, as well as life happiness, and is vital to the maintenance of intimate romantic relationships. Sexual satisfaction tends to be associated with higher levels of love, commitment, and stability in the relationship and a lower divorce rate.

Unfortunately, sexual problems, also called sexual dysfunctions, are fairly common. Research shows that in the United States, anywhere from about 10 percent to 50 percent of men, and 25 percent to 60 percent of women suffer from some form of sexual dysfunction, usually in the form of low interest in sex or difficulty achieving orgasm.

Studies found that couples who are married or in an otherwise committed relationship tend to function better sexually compared to their unattached counterparts, and those with higher educational attainment tend to have a better sex life compared to adults who achieve less educationally.

While race and ethnicity tend to have little association with the overall rate of sexual dysfunction, there seems to be some variability in the kind of dysfunction based on this demographic.

Several factors influence sexual satisfaction in women. While age can somewhat work against it, high sexual desire and satisfaction with the romantic relationship promote sexual satisfaction. Sexually satisfied women tend to have levels of sexual desire that are closely matched with those of their partner. There is some evidence that while penis length does not tend to be a factor for sexual satisfaction, penis width may very well be. Women who self-stimulate are also more likely to feel sexually satisfied. The theory there is that women who self-stimulate are more aware of their sexual wants and needs.

Communication, both generally and about one's sexual needs, is thought to be the strongest factor in achieving sexual satisfaction. Women who tend to be highly sexually assertive, like female led Queens, have higher levels of desire, orgasm ability, and sexual satisfaction compared to their nonassertive counterparts. The more often couples tend to be affectionate, both sexually and otherwise, the higher their sexual satisfaction tends to be.

Here are stats on women and having orgasms:

- 62 percent of women always orgasm during masturbation

- 34 percent of women always orgasm during oral sex

- 27 percent of women always orgasm during intercourse where the penis enters the vagina

- 26 percent of women always orgasm during genital touching

Of course, sexual satisfaction isn't just about having an orgasm, it's about the closeness and connection it brings with your partner. And, according to the survey, 60 percent of women want more intercourse. The good news is women are having sex and want more. Research shows that when we care more about our partner's sexual experience, we also report more sexual satisfaction ourselves. Further, when our partners are happy outside of the bedroom, we also experience enhanced satisfaction in the bedroom.

Individuals describing their own sexually satisfying experiences tend to say that mutual pleasure is essential to their own feelings of fulfillment. This is why it is essential to focus on serving your Queen from the moment you wake. Her mood throughout the day will determine how eager she is to have sex later in the night.

Studies also show that men who valued their partner's orgasm were more likely to report relationship happiness. This explains why men in Female Led Relationships and who focus on their Queen's pleasure experienced more happiness. The most surprising association with sexual satisfaction is when men have a feminist partner and sexual satisfaction. Research shows that men who have feminist partners report increased sexual satisfaction as well as more stable relationships, which is clear support for why Female Led Relationships work and why supporting your Queen in her journey to becoming a sex goddess will dramatically transform your relationship.

Additional Tips for Sexual Satisfaction

Below are some additional tips for sexual satisfaction to help your Queen unlock her sex goddess:

Don't Rush

Don't rush the experience. Tend to other parts of your Queen's body while you're going down on them. Tease her as you're warming them up. Instead of zeroing in on the clitoris and going to town, get the entire area wet. After some build-up, be firmer, gradually increase speed and pay attention to signs of whether there's too much stimulation or if your partner wants more.

Be Present

Being present and focused is one of the sexiest things you can ever bring to the bedroom. Be intentional about focusing on your Queen and giving her your undivided attention. Be as in the moment as possible. Presence is when you are completely there with your whole body, mind, and soul. Not distracted in thoughts or restless in your body.

Hit Her Pleasure Points

A study found that only 18 percent of women can orgasm from intercourse alone. Nearly 37 percent said clitoral stimulation was necessary for orgasm during intercourse. And 36 percent indicated that, while stimulation was not needed, their orgasms feel better if it does happen during intercourse.

So, what does this mean? Your Queen can achieve orgasm when you are doing the right things. Many women gravitate toward clitoral stimulation as a means of achieving it. Some prefer internal stimulation, more targeted toward the G-spot. There are also women who enjoy cervical stimulation, which can be delivered through deep penetration. Others prefer to access their pleasure points through anal penetration. The point is, there are a lot of different ways to make your Queen come.

Add A Lot of Kissing

Kissing creates a sense of connectedness and is the best form of foreplay. Aim for ten seconds straight every day. Once a kiss crosses the six-second mark, oxytocin is released in the brain, as is dopamine, cortisol, and a host of other hormones that get the blood pumping and the heart rate elevated. On top of the physical pleasure it produces, longer kisses can create a deep connection with your partner.

Set the Scene

Light candles. Play soft music. Do whatever is necessary to create a romantic space for you and your partner. It might sound cliché— and, sure, it is a little—but who cares? Just as a heavy metal playlist and purple light filters might hint at a different kind of sex, soft music and dim lights will set the scene for a more intimate evening, allowing you both to relax and lean into the moment.

Explore Different Positions

There are so many exciting and interesting positions to explore. Spoon position, missionary position and the lotus promote intimacy because of how the bodies are intertwined or eye contact is prioritized. The position called Oasis is very exciting. You sit on the floor, slightly leaning forward. Your legs are slightly bent at the knees and driven wide apart. Your goddess spreads her legs on both sides of your buttocks. With her arms, she hugs your neck and upper part of your back. Her body leans backward, but you hold your Queen with your hands behind her back and make the movements with her body while she rides you. The secret is the combination of deep penetration and the cradling embrace of both of you, which will exponentially increase the romance and your experience.

CHAPTER 20

Affirmations and Goddess Worship

Affirmations are becoming more popular and have significant use in many aspects of mental reprogramming for health, stress management, well-being, and now relationships. Affirmations should become an important part of goddess worship. Affirmations seem simple on the surface—just repeat a couple of lines but they are, in fact, a powerful method to control specific areas of the brain which can bring about great transformation. Many gurus and spiritual leaders swear by affirmations, which have become an important part of many programs.

For hundreds of years, the wisdom teachings of the East have utilized methods for the study and transformation of the mind-body. Mindfulness Training provides instruction in meditation, mind-body healing, and affirmations from both a psychological and spiritual perspective. Reprogramming is real and can be used in relationships.

Meditation can make your affirmations more powerful. Try meditating together with your Queen. Make it a light ritual at the beginning of your session to help to center your mind and body. Once you get into meditation and feel connected energetically, notice the subtle sensations you feel in your body. You may feel energized and a bit tingly. Now you can begin to pleasure each other while staying connected to the sensations created by your meditation. Once you are in the zone, you can add your affirmations for an even more powerful experience.

Harness sexual energy by moving it. By moving your sexual energy out of your genitals and pelvis, you distribute pleasure and goodness throughout your entire body. Rather than keeping the pleasure centered in your clitoris or the head of your penis, your whole body vibrates with pleasure.

Here are a few methods to help you start moving your sexual energy:

- **Everything begins with intention.** Set the intention to feel the subtle sensations of your sexual energy and move them. If you want the energy to move, it will. This is nothing more than imagining that it's real.

- **Sexual worship affirmations.** Affirmations can be done just lying together or during your sexual session. It can help to get you both relaxed and heightens the mood.

Use it as foreplay or during intercourse for an even more intense experience. As you repeat the lines, think deeply and focus on the pleasure you are giving to your Queen. You are attempting to excite every part of her body. Focus on the sensations, sounds, rhythms, and how she feels. Let her voice fill your entire being. Some couples choose to use these as foreplay together with roleplay and to increase the excitement. Use it in a ritual as you prepare to worship your goddess. Add some sexy massage to heighten the physical touch experience.

Many couples enjoy adding a spiritual element where sex is viewed as sacred and sexuality was seen as a positive expression of the life force. This perspective was the norm in many cultures pre-dating Greek and Roman times and these societies date back 30,000 years. Even as late as 3,500 years ago those who lived on the island of Crete recognized sexual pleasure as a wonderful way to connect with spirit, renew the abundance of the land, and unite deeply with one another. In this culture sexuality was widely understood as a pathway to spiritual ecstasy.

The fact is that sexuality and spirituality were never split until well into the first millennium of the Common Era when denial of the body became the popular theology of the day. It may seem outrageous to view sexuality in such lofty terms. Yet, it no longer makes sense to deny the spiritual dimension of our sexuality. Thomas Merton, author, said "Uninhibited erotic love between married persons, properly understood, sexual union is an expression of deep personal love and a means to the deepening, perfecting, and sanctifying of that love." Pure, sexual love can take on a quality that is sacred.

Spiritual development involving mastery of sexual energy, in the context of trusting and spiritually mature, male-female relationships, reveal the possibility of a fruitful merging of sex and spirituality. Affirmations can be used to deepen the sexual experience and merge the spiritual. Loving and feeling loved, you will feel more content, less driven, at peace within, more spontaneous as well as joyful.

Since sexual energy is the source of our connection to the life force, the benefits to physical, emotional, and mental health are obvious. Developing conscious rituals and techniques allow you to become more open to such transcendent experiences. It prepares you to be receptive to the possibility of connecting in higher states of awareness from peak sexual moments.

Here is an easy way to begin using your affirmations during sex. Start at your Queen's feet, ankles, shins, knees, thighs, hips, vagina, stomach, breasts, arms, and enjoy it very slowly. Stop at each body part and repeat a full chant four times before moving to the next body part. Go slowly and gently. Take as much time as possible on each body part. if you want, repeat multiple chants four times on each body part. You and your Queen should be in a very relaxed, open and receptive state of mind throughout the entire session. Focus your attention even more intensely on each affirmation.

When you are thinking about each affirmation, imagine how you can involve your five senses in the experience. You may use them as foreplay, or a short ritual before your lovemaking session. You may also add them during your intercourse or at the end of your session. When you are starting, it is probably best to focus on them in the beginning of your lovemaking. Begin with you both getting into a very comfortable position. In my book *Turning Point* you will find an in-depth guide to using affirmations throughout your Female Led Relationship. Here are some examples of affirmations you can use during goddess worship.

My Queen's Orgasm comes first.
(Repeat 4 Times)

I enjoy the taste, smell, and feel of my Queen's pussy.
(Repeat 4 Times)

I submit to loving and exploring my Queen's pussy.
(Repeat 4 Times)

I am becoming a pro at satisfying my Queen orally.
(Repeat 4 Times)

My Queen's oral pleasure comes first.
(Repeat 4 Times)

I will begin every sexual session connecting to my Queen's divine through oral pleasure.
(Repeat 4 Times)

My penis responds only to my Queen's command.
(Repeat 4 Times)

My penis shows my devotion to my Queen.
(Repeat 4 Times)

My penis grows rock hard and thick only for my Queen.
(Repeat 4 Times)

I remain hard and ready to serve my Queen.
(Repeat 4 Times)

Marisa Rudder

My penis is owned by my Queen.
(Repeat 4 Times)

I lust only to serve and obey my Queen.
(Repeat 4 Times)

My penis exists only to serve my Queen as much as she desires.
(Repeat 4 Times)

I serve my Queen's body with all of my energy.
(Repeat 4 Times)

I am ready and willing to do anything sexually that my Queen requests.
(Repeat 4 Times)

I place my entire trust with my Queen.
(Repeat 4 Times)

My Queen's sexual pleasure comes first.
(Repeat 4 Times)

I take care of her sexual needs, and she takes care of mine.
(Repeat 4 Times)

I focus on my Queen's sexual needs and aim to be the best at fulfilling them.
(Repeat 4 Times)

I am owned by my Queen.
(Repeat 4 Times)

My purpose is to be loyal and give proper service to my Queen.
(Repeat 4 Times)

My daily goal is to make my Queen happy.
(Repeat 4 Times)

My Queen's orgasm is more important than my own orgasm.
(Repeat 4 Times)

Sex is only for the Queen's pleasure above mine.
(Repeat 4 Times)

I ensure my Queen is sexually satisfied during each session.
(Repeat 4 Times)

She is my one and only Queen.
(Repeat 4 Times)

I am 100 percent obedient to my Queen.
(Repeat 4 Times)

CHAPTER 21

What Makes a Queen a Goddess of Love?

What makes your woman a Goddess of Love? A goddess is an otherworldly being who has power and influence over the natural world and the spiritual realm, and often symbolizes feminine qualities like beauty, love, fertility, and protection. Qualities that separate a goddess from an average woman may include but are not limited to extraordinary powers and abilities, supernatural knowledge, greater emotional and spiritual understanding, connection to a spiritual realm, and a divine and sacred presence. You may know that a woman has unlocked her inner goddess when you feel her inner strength and self-confidence radiating off of her.

You may also observe her tuning into her intuition, engaging in activities that nourish her soul, or connecting deeply to her divine femininity. You may even be able to sense her access to levels of wisdom and knowledge beyond your own understanding. A woman who has unlocked her inner goddess often becomes very aware and conscious of who she has become. She gains a deep understanding of her true self and may become more resilient, empowered, and confident. A woman who has unlocked her inner goddess may feel inspired to share her newfound knowledge and wisdom with her community, in order to create positive change and help others discover their true potential. She may also actively seek out opportunities to lend her time and energy to causes that deeply matter to her.

A woman who has unlocked her inner goddess may be focused on her goal to ensure that she leaves an indelible mark on the world. This could include leaving a legacy of empowering others to reach their full potential, making a positive impact on her community, and striving to create a lasting change for the better. A woman who has unlocked her inner goddess may be confident in her beliefs and convictions and unafraid to stand up for them. She may be empowered to openly express herself and speak out against injustice. She may be courageous in the face of adversity and challenging situations.

Additionally, a woman who has unlocked her inner goddess does not necessarily have to be self-sufficient. She may recognize her personal strengths and weaknesses as well as recognize strengths and weaknesses in her relationships with others to create a supportive and empowering system. Some women may rely on support from others, either through friendship, guidance, or other forms of assistance.

A woman who has unlocked her inner goddess may be all of these things. Kindness is about being considerate and thoughtful in how you interact with other people. Confidence is believing in your own abilities and having faith in yourself. Being inspiring is motivating others and cultivating creative ideas. Boldness is having the courage to take risks and go after what you want. Truthfulness is being honest and sincere when speaking or acting. Dedication is putting in the work and commitment to achieving your goals. Honesty is being truthful and genuine in how you interact with others.

Compassion

A woman who has unlocked her inner goddess may use compassion as a powerful tool. Compassion involves understanding others, feeling empathy, and being understanding. It encourages treating others with kindness, respect, and love. Compassion can be used to connect with others and inspire greater understanding, peace, and love.

Goddesses Never Stop Learning

A woman who has unlocked her inner goddess does not stop learning or placing a high value on self-improvement. She may focus on different areas of her life, such as spiritual development or self-care, but she will always be striving to become the best version of herself. She will have an open mind to new ideas and understanding, and she will value the process of continual self-improvement.

High Self-Esteem

A woman who has unlocked her inner goddess is likely to carry herself in a confident, positive way and will have high self-esteem. She will be empowered in her own skin, able to identify her own strengths and weaknesses, and will take care of her mental and physical health. She will be passionate about creating positive change in her own life, and the lives of those around her.

Great Communication Skills

You will notice that a woman who has unlocked her inner goddess is likely to have above-average communication skills, and will be comfortable discussing feelings, thoughts, and opinions with a variety of people. She will not be afraid to express her opinion in a respectful and engaging manner, and she will be confident in engaging in conversations to reach the desired outcome.

Goddesses Don't Surrender

A woman who has unlocked her inner goddess will still have dreams and goals to strive for. She will have the confidence to pursue these dreams and a new sense of motivation to achieve them. If she falls, she will rise again. A gentleman can play an important role in helping a woman who has unlocked her inner goddess achieve her goals. He can provide support and encouragement that can help her keep striving toward her goals. He can also help her find resources and information to assist her in her journey. There is real growth in your union, which is why a Female Led Relationship or female led marriage is such an enriching and transformative experience.

CHAPTER 22

Smash the Patriarchy

Women have endured centuries of abuse, mistreatment, control, and dissatisfaction. Laws were enacted to prevent women from inheriting, owning property, and living their lives freely. They are taught from birth the importance of making the man happy and never rebel against the status quo. Over a century ago the patriarchy sought to destroy the world of goddesses. Women who were freely connected to the divine were deemed witches and many were killed in the most gruesome of ways—drowned, burned, hung, and stoned. Goddess worship was condemned by the Catholic church and people were conditioned to believe that it was the work of the devil. For years, people were afraid of this negative connotation.

Patriarchy began to destroy goddess worship in the Iron Age (1200–600 BC) during the transition from a matriarchal to a patriarchal religious and social system. During this period, the male gods of the ancient Mesopotamian and Greek pantheon began to be worshipped, leading to the diminishment of the goddess worship and their connection to Divine Feminine energy and power. The patriarchy continued to thrive in the following centuries, leading to goddess worship becoming regarded as heretical in many parts of the world.

Christianity was an especially significant tool used in the destruction of goddess worship. Christianity denigrated goddess worship as pagan and a form of sinful idolatry, and systematically supported reinterpretations of ancient female deities into new Christian saints, or else they chose to demonize them as evil entities. This helped to erase goddess worship from the cultural landscape and undercut the system of feminine power and leadership that many goddess-worshipping cultures had relied upon. Patriarchal cultures tried to use this switch to control women and limit their economic, social, and religious power. The Church also persecuted and condemned (and often burned or executed) women who continued to practice goddess-centered spirituality or attempted to pass down stories, rituals, or other symbols associated with pre-Christian spirituality. Islam, like Christianity, was also instrumental in the destruction of goddess worship.

Islamic scriptures taught that polytheism was wrong and strictly forbade the worship of female deities or goddesses. Unlike Christianity, however, Islam did not create doctored "sacred" versions of pre-Islamic creatures or beliefs; instead, it simply wiped them out by condemning their religious practices. As a result, many of the matriarchal, goddess-worshipping societies of the Middle East, Asia, and Africa were largely eradicated or drastically altered in the wake of Islamic propagation and expansion. Furthermore, many women today who live under the auspices of Islam face a restrictive form of patriarchal leadership and gender roles, with women often forbidden from speaking in public or wearing certain clothing.

A goddess frightens patriarchal men because they know a woman can use the art of seduction to make a gentleman become obsessed with her majesty, grace. This puts men at the mercy of women. However, in loving Female Led Relationships, women show mercy to men when they lack respect, obedience, or fail to serve properly. Patriarchal men are afraid of goddess worship and the Divine Feminine because they fear a loss of power and control. Worshipping goddesses, who are traditionally seen as representing female strength, is seen as a challenge to traditional male power structures and norms.

Worshipping the Divine Feminine is often seen as a form of resistance, particularly in communities and cultures which place a focus on male patriarchs and power holders. In this way, some patriarchal men may see goddess worship as becoming a threat to their social, political, and financial power and status. Additionally, goddess worship may be seen as a rejection of traditional male-dominated religions and beliefs, furthering this patriarchal fear of loss of control in society. But today, women are embracing their inner goddess and females are becoming more powerful.

It is important to keep progressing by smashing the patriarchy. Patriarchy means "rule of the father," from the ancient Greek. Allen Johnson, researcher, said, "A society is patriarchal to the degree that it is male-dominated, male-identified, and male-centered. The reality of male dominance is clearly seen in the fact that positions of authority are generally held by men or even reserved for men only. Patriarchal societies are male-identified in that the core cultural ideas about what is good, desirable, preferable, or normal are associated with how we think about men and masculinity."

What we learn is that patriarchy is generally not an explicit ongoing effort by men to dominate women. It is a long-standing system that we are born into and participate in, mostly unconsciously. Patriarchy is generally not an explicit ongoing effort by men to dominate women. It is a long-standing system that we are born into and participate in, mostly unconsciously. While most people in a patriarchal hierarchy accept their place in the pecking order, those who do not are generally dealt with by ridicule, coercion, and even violence where necessary.

Men often deny the existence or at least the power of patriarchy because they do not feel a sense of freedom, a sense of real powerfulness within the system. The truth is that it constricts and restrains everyone, not just the people at the very bottom of its hierarchy. Now that we have defined the contemporary manifestation of this ancient way of being, and maybe understand how it has managed to perpetuate itself through a couple hundred generations of parents to children, how then do we address challenges and working toward ending this? The *Love and Obey* movement breaks the "gender barrier" by turning everything around. Males submit to females and your goal is to learn to serve your Queen and support her evolution into goddess.

In the past, women were forced to learn how to please to the exclusion of their own desires. Men have deliberately tried to control women because they have known for centuries, hundreds of years, even millennia, thousands of years that female sexuality is one of the most powerful and dangerous forces in the universe. Something that needs to be controlled by men, physically, legally, religiously, and socially. It is written that all the way back to the Garden of Eden and the very first woman, Eve, our female sexuality is the cause of original sin and all of man's problems. Women are encouraged to be modest and abstain from sex and so many legends of sirens who possess female sexual power exist. La Xtabay, the siren of the Yucatan, who is described in Mayan folklore as a demonic femme fatale who preys upon men in the forests of the Yucatan Peninsula. She is said to lure men to their deaths with her incomparable beauty.

In other legends, Lamia had an affair with Zeus, and as a punishment, Hera killed her children or made Lamia kill them. Either way she was transformed into a monstrous child murderer. It has been suggested that Lamia is designated as a monster because she represents male fears about women failing to live up to the patriarchal standards of motherhood or rejecting this role entirely. Medusa's story explores female dynamics, female power against patriarchal forces, and the ultimate defense against the male gaze. Medusa was the emblem of female power back in Ancient Greece and a symbol of both protection and aggression.

And of course, Helen of Troy called "Helen the Whore," and the curse of beauty. It is her part as a fantasy whore because she had many sexual partners. She was said to have "the face that launched a thousand ships." She is remembered, judged, and hated by every age for more than 2,700 years. If you are a woman and are sexual, you will be remembered, loved, judged, and hated by men. The power of female beauty and sexuality creates great resentment. All women are sirens, imbued with great power. Capable of experiencing and delivering immense pleasure to men, but also catastrophic pain.

Patriarchy has been in place since ancient times. It is the result of the gender power dynamics, which men have historically used to gain control of political and social systems, falsely claiming their superiority to women. The patriarchy has been in power since at least 3,000 BC, when the Ancient Egyptians instituted a patriarchal social structure. The good news is the patriarchal system is slowly dying out in the modern world due to a variety of factors. The rising importance of gender and race equality, along with the changing nature of the family structure, have made the traditional notion of patriarchy increasingly irrelevant. Additionally, women are becoming more empowered and are more likely to pursue their own goals and ambitions, with the rise of female leadership in business, politics, and other areas. All of these factors are contributing to a decline in the influence of patriarchy in modern times, and the emergence of new social structures, including matriarchy.

In a matriarchal system, women generally have a greater say in decision-making and power dynamics than men, though of course the exact extent of their power will vary from situation to situation. Generally, the focus is on collaboration with both genders respected and heard in the decision-making processes. A matriarchal system is often seen as being more equitable, as it places importance on the contributions and decisions of both men and women, rather than privileging one gender over the other. This system encourages open communication between genders and has the potential to reduce gender roles and stereotypes.

In addition, this system puts a greater emphasis on balancing the responsibilities for both family and career, benefiting both men and women. Therefore, a matriarchal system is more beneficial than a patriarchal system, as it promotes both gender equality and mutual respect. The reason women make better leaders than men is because women are more empathetic and supportive, possess better communication and emotional intelligence skills, and have a more open and collaborative style of leadership. Women often have the ability to make decisions more objectively while maintaining an inclusive and balanced approach. Today, even previously patriarchal corporations feel that the presence of a female leader can encourage gender diversity throughout the company, helping to create an environment where both men and women can thrive.

In *Love and Obey*, the concept of a goddess is complex and open to personal interpretation. We view the goddess as a vessel of the universe's interconnected forms of energy. She is constantly in motion and in flux. A goddess is a divine or enlightened woman who exists outside of patriarchal and social rules. She follows her own guidance on how to live in love, peace, and harmony within her female led world. An important part of empowering your woman is goddess worship and how well you understand how to worship her correctly makes all the difference in your female led life.

Made in the USA
Las Vegas, NV
02 May 2023

71449198R00103